D1302542

DATE DUE

Foreign Capital
for Economic
Development

New York University
CENTER FOR INTERNATIONAL STUDIES

Studies in Peaceful Change

WHY FEDERATIONS FAIL: An Inquiry into the Requisites for Successful Federalism
Thomas M. Franck, Gisbert H. Flanz, Herbert J. Spiro and Frank N. Trager
New York: New York University Press, 1968

A FREE TRADE ASSOCIATION
Thomas M. Franck and Edward Weisband (eds.)
New York: New York University Press, 1968

COMPARATIVE CONSTITUTIONAL PROCESS
Thomas M. Franck
New York: Frederick A. Praeger, Inc.; London: Sweet & Maxwell Ltd., 1968

THE STRUCTURE OF IMPARTIALITY
Thomas M. Franck
New York: The Macmillan Company, 1968

AGENTS OF CHANGE: A Close Look at the Peace Corps
David Hapgood and Meridan Bennett
Boston: Little, Brown and Company, 1968

LAW, REASON AND JUSTICE: Essays in Legal Philosophy
Graham B. Hughes
New York: New York University Press, 1969

CZECHOSLOVAKIA: Intervention and Impact
I. William Zartman (ed.)
New York: New York University Press, 1970

SIERRA LEONE: An Experiment in Democracy in an African Nation
Gershon Collier
New York: New York University Press, 1970

MICROSTATES AND MICRONESIA: Problems of America's Pacific Islands and Other Minute Territories
Stanley A. de Smith
New York: New York University Press, 1970

INTERNATIONAL BUSINESS NEGOTIATIONS: A Study in India
Ashok Kapoor
New York: New York University Press, 1970

PRAEGER SPECIAL STUDIES IN
INTERNATIONAL ECONOMICS AND DEVELOPMENT

Foreign Capital for Economic Development

A KOREAN CASE STUDY

Seung Hee Kim

Foreword by
Thomas M. Franck

Studies in Peaceful Change

**Prepared Under the Auspices of
The Center for International Studies,
New York University**

PRAEGER PUBLISHERS
New York • Washington • London

The purpose of Praeger Special Studies is to make specialized research in U.S. and international economics and politics available to the academic, business, and government communities. For further information, write to the Special Projects Division, Praeger Publishers, Inc., 111 Fourth Avenue, New York, N.Y. 10003.

PRAEGER PUBLISHERS
111 Fourth Avenue, New York, N.Y. 10003, U.S.A.
5, Cromwell Place, London S.W.7, England

Published in the United States of America in 1970
by Praeger Publishers, Inc.

Library of Congress Catalog Card Number: 73-126779

Printed in the United States of America

FOREWORD

The "Studies in Peaceful Change" series of the
Center for International Studies of New York University are directed toward the analysis and exploration
of avenues of peaceful social change in an international context. One of the most important aspects of
peaceful change among developing countries, as has
been repeatedly emphasized by UNCTAD, is the evolu-
tionary but rapid transition to modern industrial
economic societies.

International aid and private investment from
the developing countries is one avenue by which this
transition may be accelerated. But, as spokesmen for
the recipient nations are quick to point out, aid and
private investment carry their own dangers--such as
adding to an already heavy foreign debt-service
burden or exploiting the nations' irreplaceable natural resources.

Korea, which received large amounts of both economic and military aid from the United States in the
1950's and early 1960's, has been cited as one of the
success stories of the U.S. aid program. Together
with only a few other countries (e.g., Taiwan and
Turkey), Korea has "turned the corner," and official
economic aid has been phased out while economic expansion and rising export receipts appear to be pro-
pelling the economy on a course of self-sustained
development.

In the present volume, Seung Hee Kim adds considerably to our understanding of the reasons for
Korea's "success." He examines the process by which
official aid was translated into exports and import
substitutes in order to provide the means to service
a rising external debt. He goes further in order to
project the future capital inflows needed both to

ratify Korea's past boom and to convert the country from a capital importer to a net capital exporter. In the process, he estimates the dollars needed to pay interest and principal on debt incurred in the past and how this figure declines in the future.

Building on the studies of others, Professor Kim analyzes the contribution of foreign capital and aid to Korea's economic development over the past fifteen years, and thereafter projects the amount of additional foreign capital needed to sustain similar development for the next decade. More specifically, the study examines several economic relationships: the relationship between investment and output, i.e., the "incremental capital-output ratio"; the relationship of domestic savings in Korea with national income and the distribution of income; the relationship between required imports and potential production; and the relationship between exports and Korean policies relating to export promotion. In each case, the influences of past government policies on the observed relationships are analyzed. These include foreign exchange policies, commercial policies, and financial policies.

Professor Kim's study is uniquely comprehensive in that it includes the efforts of import substitution-policies as well as future debt service payments in its estimates of the needs for foreign capital in the next decade. The usual "two gap" analysis of external resource needs for development is thereby extended to the level of the individual policy measures of one country. One result is the illumination of the Korean "showcase" of United States foreign aid.

Thomas M. Franck, Director
Center for International Studies
New York University

PREFACE

Foreign capital is a subject of increasing importance not only in capital-importing countries but also in capital-exporting countries. For the advanced capital-exporting countries, foreign investment in less-developed countries is becoming a new area of exploration, as developing countries continue to grow and participate in world export markets. For the capital-importing countries, foreign capital is the primary source of economic development and modern technology.

And yet, most foreign direct investment has been flowing into Europe and the West, and only a marginal amount has been going into developing countries. The bulk of foreign capital in developing countries such as South Korea is in the form of external debt, mainly because political and financial risks make advanced countries reluctant to invest directly in less-developed countries, and partly because the host countries have shown a dangerously emotional, nationalistic attitude toward foreign investment.

In recent years, the burden of external debts, including amortization and interest payments, has greatly increased in developing countries. Consequently, there is a question as to whether a borrowing country can afford to accumulate and pay back external debts in the future. Thus, there is a great need for an analytical tool to evaluate the creditworthiness of a borrowing country. The days of a "beggar-thy-neighbor" type of foreign aid are fading, and the future analysis of debt-servicing capacity will be based on the borrowing country's economic strength.

The intention of this book is to design a theory of foreign capital relevant to developing countries in general and to the Republic of Korea in particular. Although Korea encourages the inflow of foreign capital, the government arbitrarily limits the amount of external debt according to the ratio of debt-service costs to export earnings. The debt-service ratio shows only one aspect of a short-run liquidity problem. A simultaneous, dynamic assessment of all factors determining debt-servicing capacity in the long run is more important than the absolute size of debt-service requirements.

This study attempts to integrate the factors that affect the amount of foreign-capital needs in Korea and the forces that determine the parameter values of these factors. The major economic factors discussed in this book are aggregate income, investment, savings, exports, and imports. The major financial factors are money supply, interest rates, foreign-exchange reserves, terms of trade, foreign-exchange rates, and interest and amortization payments on the country's external debts.

This book is a revised and statistically updated version of the author's doctoral dissertation. A great deal of research was done while the author was a Junior Fellow at the Center for International Studies, New York University. He is grateful to Thomas Franck, Director of the Center, who created an intellectual atmosphere through open discussion of the subject. It was also the privilege of the author to work under the guidance of Peter G. Franck, a Visiting Senior Fellow at the Center.

While writing his dissertation, the author appreciated the help of faculty members at the New York University Graduate School of Business Administration. In particular, Robert G. Hawkins, chairman of the doctoral committee, suggested ways to approach, analyze, and organize the economic problems involved in the study. Without his sincere help and untiring encouragement, this study could not have been completed. Professor Hawkins, Halger L. Engberg, and G. Narasimham (all of the Center for International Studies) have offered valuable comments and criticism.

During his research period, the author was fortunate to have had interviews with people too numerous to be mentioned in this limited space. Special thanks are due the following institutions, which provided expert information and rare source materials for the book: the Economic and Scientific Advisory Council of the President of the Republic of Korea, the Bank of Korea, the Korea Exchange Bank, the International Bank for Reconstruction and Development (IBRD), the International Monetary Fund (IMF), the Agency for International Development (AID), the Korean Embassy in Washington, D.C., the Ministry of Finance of Korea, the Ministry of Commerce and Industry of Korea, the Library of the Federal Reserve Bank of New York, and the United Nations Library.

Furthermore, the author is deeply grateful to the Graduate School of Business Administration, New York University, for generous financial assistance through the Von Mises and Marcus Nadler fellowships.

Finally, Mary C. Mone, Editor, Praeger Special Studies, read the manuscript and made suggestions for revising the study. The author, of course, takes full responsibility for any errors that may remain.

Seung Hee Kim

CONTENTS

xi

LIST OF TABLES

xiv

LIST OF FIGURES

LIST OF ABBREVIATIONS*

AA	automatic-approval list
AID	Agency for International Development
AOD	annual increase in outstanding debt
CD's	certificates of time deposits
CEB	Combined Economic Board
COD	cumulative outstanding debts
D	net borrowing
D/A	document against acceptance
DI	direct investment
D/P	document against payment
DS	debt-service requirements
EEC	European Economic Community
EK	external-capital needs
ECAFE	United Nations Economic Commission for Asia and the Far East
FK	foreign-capital needs
GATT	General Agreement on Tariffs and Trade

---

*For additional abbreviations, also see Chapter 1, Summary, as well as Chapter 2, Table 2.17.

GD	new gross borrowing
GDP	gross domestic product
GNP	gross national product
IBRD	International Bank for Reconstruction and Development
ICOR	incremental capital-output ratio
IMF	International Monetary Fund
LDC's	less-developed countries
P	prohibited items
PLD	public debt
PRD	private debt
R	restricted items
RRS	region of recent settlement
SITC	Standard International Trade Classification
SR	semirestricted items
T	transfer payments
UNCTAD	United Conference on Trade and Development
UNKRA	U.N. Korean Reconstruction Agency
USOM	U.S. Overseas Mission

INTRODUCTION

There are many important factors affecting
economic development in developing countries. In
Korea, the most important are manpower, foreign capital, and technology. Foreign capital has been
chosen by economic planners as the major source of
economic development in Korea, where labor is generally abundant, and domestic savings are relatively low.
Furthermore, foreign capital is the primary source
of new, modern equipment and technical assistance.

Foreign capital has helped Korea to rise above
a low level of income. Before 1957, most of the
foreign capital in Korea had been foreign aid in the
form of government grants, mainly from the United
States. The nature of foreign aid changed in 1957,
when U.S. foreign-aid policy shifted its emphasis
from grants to development-loan programs. At present, loans from the United States, Japan, and Germany
are the major sources of foreign capital in Korea.

The growth-oriented new government has encouraged the influx of foreign capital. Under the present law, however, an application for the inducement
of foreign capital must be approved by the Korean
Government in order to meet basic requirements for
the development program. The repayment of external
debt, including principal and interest, is guaranteed
by the government, whether the ultimate lenders in
private loans are foreign private enterprises or
those in public loans are public institutions such as
the U.S. Agency for International Development (AID),
the World Bank, and other foreign governments.[1]

The amount of foreign capital has increased
vastly in recent years. The first external debt in
Korea was the public loan of $2 million in 1959 to
the Oriental Cement Company for AID's Development

Loan Fund.[2] External debt amounted to only $5 million in 1960. At the end of 1968, total accumulated public loans amounted to $477 million, private loans amounted to $939 million, and foreign direct investments to $92 million.[3]

Although the rapid economic growth in recent years has been possible with the help of external debt, the latter results in the problem of debt-service payments. Actual debt-service payments, including interest as well as amortization, increased from $1.1 million in 1962 to $51.8 million in 1968.[4]

The problem will become severe as the grace period on some of the external debt ends and debt service accumulates in the future. The Korean Government must realize the consequences of rising external debt. In the event of default, Korea will lose her international credit standing and jeopardize her future economic-development planning, which relies heavily on foreign capital. In short, an evaluation of Korea's ability to pay back external debt is not only desirable but of paramount importance.

The main topic of this book is an estimate of foreign-capital needs in Korea. No one disagrees with the idea that an inflow of foreign capital is desirable and needed to help finance economic development in countries such as Korea. However, there are several areas of disagreement. First, what is the size of foreign-capital needs in Korea? Is it $1 billion or $1 million a year, and on what basis is this amount determined? Second, how long is the dependence on foreign capital in Korea going to last? Finally, will she be able to pay back her external debt without default?

In this study, a theoretical model is designed that permits an estimate of foreign-capital needs in Korea. The theory postulates that foreign-capital needs are a function of aggregate income, investment, savings, imports, exports, foreign-exchange reserves, and interest and amortization on the country'x external debts.

The theoretical framework is developed and compared with recent contributions by other economists to the subject of foreign-capital needs in developing countries. Our model consists of the aggregate economic variables in contrast to sectoral variables. The aggregate model is more appropriate in the case of Korea than the sectoral model simply because it is much more difficult to estimate sectoral parameter values. Detailed data on interindustry relationships are generally neither available nor reliable in developing countries such as Korea.

The theory is then applied to Korea by estimating foreign-capital needs with given parameters. In order to estimate the parameters, the past performance of the major factors affecting relevant parameters is analyzed in detail and depth, and an assessment of likely future courses in these factors is made for the projection. For example, in analyzing the factors affecting exports, not only cost factors but also international-demand conditions are discussed. The major factors affecting imports are considered to be industrialization and import substitution. Furthermore, financial and fiscal techniques to increase domestic savings are studied. Finally, government policies to promote exports and savings and policies to establish investment and import plans are evaluated.

NOTES

1. The Status Report of Foreign Capital Inflow by Projects (Seoul: Economic Planning Board, 1967), p. 3.

2. Ibid., pp. 3-5.

3. Review of Korean Economy, 1968 (Seoul: Bank of Korea, 1969), p. 145.

4. Ibid., p. 146.

Foreign Capital
for Economic
Development

CHAPTER **1** THE THEORY OF EXTERNAL-
CAPITAL REQUIREMENTS

INTRODUCTION

The main thrust of this chapter is a detailed analysis of the theory of external-capital needs in developing countries such as Korea. Although recent contributions[1] have been made to a general theory of external capital needs in the course of economic development, a theory that may be most appropriate to Korea is formulated here. It consists of the theories of the internal gap, the external gap, debt services on external debts, and foreign-exchange reserve. This chapter thus combines several theories postulated in other studies.

The reason for dealing with the theories of both internal and external gaps is the ex ante inequality of the two gaps. Ex post, they are always identical.

In terms of the internal gap, foreign-capital needs (FK) can be expressed as

$$FK = I_r - S_d \tag{1}$$

where I_r is total investment required to achieve the output target, and S_d is potential domestic savings. Most studies on foreign-capital needs have focused on estimating the need for foreign capital to achieve a "target" growth rate. In order to keep that form, these studies tend to oversimplify the problems that arise in formulating appropriate capital-output ratios and aggregate-savings functions.

The external gap can also be expressed as

$$FK = M_r - X \qquad (2)$$

where M_r and X stand for total import requirements
and potential export earnings, respectively. This
formulation postulates a required relationship of imports to total output and an exogenously determined
level of exports.

Foreign debt-service requirements (DS) can also
be obtained by specifying the average interest rate
and repayment period of future as well as past external debts. In addition, it may be expected that
the foreign-exchange reserve should grow as development proceeds. The change in reserve d(FK) can be
obtained conveniently by relating the level of
foreign-exchange reserve to trade volume. Thus, total
external capital needs (EK), including debt services,
and the change in foreign reserve, are defined as

$$EK = FK + DS + d\ (FX) \qquad (3)$$

where FK is either the internal gap or external gap.

The ex post internal gap is always equal to the
ex post external gap in national-income accounting,

$$Y = C + I + (X - M) \qquad (4a)$$

where Y and C stand for total output and consumption,
respectively.

In equation (4a), the ex post internal gap is
$I - (Y-C)$, while the ex post external gap is M - X.
Since (Y-C) is domestic savings, we have

$$I - S_d = M - X \qquad (4b)$$

where the left-hand side of the equation is the internal gap, while the right-hand side is the external
gap. Hence, identity of two ex post gaps is achieved.[2]

However, the ex ante internal and external gaps
may not be equal because the functional relationship

of each gap is differently specified. The inequality of the two gaps is similar to the inequality between the ex ante savings and ex ante investment in
Keynesian aggregate-income analysis. It must be
shown, then, how ex post equality between the two
gaps is achieved.

THEORY OF THE INTERNAL GAP

The internal gap, given a target for the gross
national product (GNP), is the difference between
the required investment (I_r) to achieve the target
output (Y) and the savings generated domestically
(S_d) at Y. The relationships between I and Y and S
and Y are examined in this section.

At the outset, real gross national product (Y)
is assumed to increase at a target rate of growth,
r percent per annum over the period. Then, the target output (Y) in the nth year is

$$(Y)_n = Y_o (1 + r)^n \qquad (5)$$

where real income grows at a compound rate starting
from the base year (Y_o).

Our growth formula can be compared with other
economists' equations. The equation of Hollis B.
Chenery and A. M. Strout is almost identical with
ours. Their growth equation is $Y_n = Y_{n-1} (1 + r)$.[3]
D. Avramovic uses Y for gross domestic product (GDP).[4]
The discrepancy between GDP and GNP may be insignif-
icant if net-factor income from the rest of the world
is negligible. Jaroslav Vanek, on the other hand,
projects the values added of eight sectors of the
economy, and they add up to GNP at factor cost as
shown in $V = (V_1 + V_2 + . . . + V_8)$. Note that
$V = GNP$; V_1, V_2, and so forth = value added by each
of eight sectors.

The extremely complex relationships between investment and output have often been summarized in the
capital-output ratio (k), which may be treated as a
constant or a variable. Thus, the relationship can

be shown as

$$I_r = k(Y) \qquad (6a)$$

or required investment is a constant (k) times the target output. The relationships can also be expressed:

$$(I_r)_n = kr\,(Y_o)\,(1+r)^n \qquad (6b)$$

by substituting equation (5) for Y in equation (6a). The investment function shows that total-investment requirements in the nth year are a constant fraction of the total income in the nth year. Investment is used here as a gross figure and includes depreciation.

Most aggregate investment functions are very similar to our investment function. These other equations are: $I = krY$ by Rosenstein-Rodan and $I_n = k(Y_{n+1} - Y_n)$ by Avramovic. Vanek, however, divides total investment into several sectors, $(I = I_1 + I_2 + \ldots + I_i)$, and sectoral-investment requirements are obtained by multiplying the incremental capital-output ratio of a sector (k_i) with a target growth of a sector (V_i); i.e., $I_i = k_i(V_i)$.[5]

Treatment of the capital-output ratio (k) in a growth context goes back to Harrod and Domar whose models form the essential basis for the internal-gap theory.[6] The incremental capital-output ratio can be expressed as

$$k = \frac{dK}{dY} = \frac{I}{dY} \qquad (7a)$$

which shows the identity between the ratio of the change in capital to the change in total income and the ratio of investment to change in total income. For growth models, the marginal rather than the average capital-output ratio is the relevant one.

The incremental capital-output ratio in the nth year (k_n) can also be expressed with a one-period lag between investment and additional income,

$$k_n = \frac{I_n}{Y_n - Y_{n-1}} \tag{7b}$$

and the average incremental capital-output ratio $(\bar{k})$ is

$$\bar{k} = \frac{1}{n} (k_1 + k_2 \ldots + k_n). \tag{7c}$$

A relevant savings function is also difficult to formulate. Rosenstein-Rodan, Avramovic, and Chenery and Strout all assume savings to be a linear function of real income, i.e., $S = a + b (Y)$.[7] Thus, following their lead, in our saving function total domestic savings in the nth year is the sum of savings in the base year and marginal savings in subsequent years. Explicitly,

$$S_n = s(Y_o) + \sum_{n=1}^{n} s' \left[Y_o (1 + r)^n - Y_o (1 + r)^{n-1} \right] \tag{8}$$

where s and s' are the average- and marginal-savings rates, respectively. It is generally believed that s' is--or has to be--larger than s. Rosenstein-Rodan has made a persuasive argument that "a marginal rate considerably higher than the average rate is the main lever of economic development in underdeveloped countries."[8]

The internal gap, as noted before, is the difference between the investment required for the target output (Y) and domestic savings. Substituting the investment function equation (6b), and the savings function, equation (8), into equation (1) to obtain the final form of internal gap, it becomes

$$FK = \left[kr (Y_o) \cdot (1 + r)^n \right] - \left[s(Y_o) + \sum_{n=1}^{n} s' \left\{ Y_o (1+r)^n - Y_o (1 + r)^{n-1} \right\} \right] \tag{9}$$

In deriving the internal gap, Rosenstein-Rodan and Fei and Paauw employ a fixed incremental capital-output ratio in estimating the future investment requirements necessary to permit target rates of

output to be achieved.[9] A fixed incremental capital-
output ratio, e.g., of 3:1, implies that a one-unit
increase in output requires three additional units
of capital stock, and this ratio is assumed to stay
constant over time. If we in addition assume a target growth rate in output, e.g., r of 5 percent, the
required rate of investment is kr percent or 15 percent of GNP.

The fixed incremental capital-output ratio implies parallel growth of investment and total output.
In reality, however, investment and total output may
not increase over any period as a whole at exactly
the same rate--i.e., the incremental capital-output
ratio may not be stable. This is why a fixed or
average incremental capital-output ratio has limited
practical applicability in estimating actual investment requirements; and this assumption is persistent-
ly and correctly criticized. Some economists criticize the fixed capital-output ratio because of the
claim that the significance of noncapital inputs affecting growth has been greater than that of capital
investments.[10]

However, Vanek, although he realizes the inherent
instability of the gross capital-output ratio, nevertheless considers it one of the most useful tools of
analysis in developing countries.[11] Vanek justifies
the assumption of fixed capital-output ratio as
follows:

> It can only be hypothesized that if the
> period over which predictions are sought
> is sufficiently short [10-15 years], a
> given volume of additional output [nation-
> al or sectoral] will require a proportion-
> al increase in total capital stock, the
> factor of proportionality between incre-
> ments in output and net capital formation
> being at least approximately unchanged.
> The rationale behind this notion [especial-
> ly for the less developed countries] is
> either that technology is subject to fixed
> coefficients and labor really is not a
> scarce factor; or that if capital-labor

substitution actually takes place, the
law of diminishing marginal return is
offset by gradual increases in technology; or that both factors cooperate in
producing a comparative stability of the
net capital-output coefficient.[12]

Chenery and Strout further argue that the assumption of a linear capital-output function is a
matter of convenience and assume that the absorptive
capacity for investment will grow at the same rate as
investment itself. They say that labor and manageri-
al skills are not the limiting factors in many developing countries. They also argue that the introduction of a nonlinear relation between capital and
output would not materially affect their analysis,
for they employ both high and low values of k.[13]

In short, then, a fixed capital-output ratio is
useful--if properly understood as an approximation--
in formulating an investment function. Consequently,
the assumption of a fixed incremental capital-output
ratio is helpful in a case such as Korea, where data
on productivity, factor substitution, and the absorptive capacity are very difficult to obtain. It is
impossible to find another operational tool for which
satisfactory data would be available. Therefore, a
fixed ratio with high and low values is used in this
study as a proxy for investment requirements, although it is recognized that the implicit assumptions
regarding other factors that affect the ratio may not
be correct. The fixed ratio is the key to estimating
investment requirements which are one of the two components in the internal gap. The other component is
savings.

There are some types of savings function other
than the aggregate function stated above. Fei and
Paauw formulate their savings function on a per-
capita basis but also as a constant fraction of the
increment on per-capita income. Explicitly, per-
capita savings (S*) are the sum of per-capita average
savings, s(Y*) in the base year and per-capita marginal savings in subsequent years, u(dY*/dt). Thus,
the saving function becomes $S* = s(Y_0^*) + u(Y^*)$.[14]

The aggregate and per-capita methods will produce
identical results if the aggregate-average savings
rate is equal to the per-capita average savings rate
and the aggregate marginal savings rate is equal to
the per-capita marginal savings rate. Per-capita
savings are nothing but total savings divided by
population.

A rather different savings function is specified by Vanek, who divides total savings into several
components, such as depreciation of fixed capital,
corporate savings and taxes, and government and household savings.[15] Each component of total savings is
in turn functionally related to the income of the
productive sectors of the economy and/or independent
variables. For instance, S_{cp}, corporate savings and
taxes, is a function of the values added of sectors
2,3,4, S_{cp} = .24 $V_{2,3,4}$, while S_{gh}, government and
household savings, is a function of GNP(V) and terms
of trade (T), S_{gh} = V(0.095 - 0.0238).[16]

Vanek originally composed his savings function
by functional sectors of the economy. But he aban-
doned the endeavor partly because the usefulness of
such an approach is dubious in developing countries
and partly because such sectoral data do not exist.

Even Vanek's savings function is in practice
inferior to an aggregate-savings function. Some components of Vanek's function depend on the values
added by several sectors of the economy, while aggregate savings depend on total GNP. It is difficult
to project values added by different sectors simply
because the industrial structure of the economy
changes as it grows. Not only the savings rate but
the capital-output ratio and the sensitivity to
foreign-capital needs of a sector may vary significantly as "the relative sizes of the various sectors
change in different stages of economic development."[17]
The direct and indirect effects of changing industrial structure among different sectors are submerged
in an aggregate analysis, which is a more feasible
operational procedure.

The underlying problem is, of course, that the
calculation of values added by various sectors of the

economy is difficult, because the available input-
output table is very crude and not reliable. Consequently, the aggregate approach is necessary due to
time and resource limitations. Furthermore, the values added by broad sectors include the interindustry
flows, and "equilibrium factor prices cannot be determined at the micro-economic level; they are a
function of developments in the over-all economy."[18]
Even though the micro or sectoral analysis neglects
the interrelationships among sectors, the aggregate
approach takes account of "direct and indirect effects,
external and internal economies as well as the portion
of income stream generated by the initial investment
which is saved and reinvested."[19]

THEORY OF THE EXTERNAL GAP

A theory of the external gap is required since,
as noted earlier, the ex ante external gap may not
be equal to the ex ante internal gap.[20] The external
gap is essentially a foreign-goods shortage. It
rests on a postulated relationship between imports
for Y and potential exports. Imports require foreign
exchange, and the only sources of foreign exchange
are exports of goods and services or FK. The latter
is, of course, our object of concern.

In the typical model, imports are related to
GNP and to an import-substitution coefficient. The
usual formulation of the import function without the
substitution coefficient is $M = a + b (Y)$, where M
is the dependent variable.[21] However, external-gap
theory makes the causal relationship bidirectional.
In order to reach Y, M* is a minimum requirement

$$M^*_n = m (Y_n). \tag{10a}$$

Through time and with the progress of industrialization, the range of essential import goods will be
reduced by the output of new domestic industries.
This process of import substitution will tend to lower
the coefficient (m) relating M* and Y, if the supply
of import substitutes produced domestically exceeds
the demand for imports.[22] For Korea, import substitution has been and will continue to be such an important

factor that to ignore it would reduce the usefulness
of empirical estimates. However, most external-gap
estimates have ignored this factor.

Therefore, required imports (M*) are the net effect of two opposing forces, namely potential imports
(M_p) and import substitutes (M_s), explicitly. (M*
designates imports of goods and services excluding
interest on external debts.)

$$M^* = M_p - M_s, \qquad (10b)$$

Potential imports are assumed to be a fraction
of total output (Y) in the nth year,

$$M_p = m_1 (Y_n), \qquad (10c)$$

where m_1 shows the degree of dependence on foreign
goods and services.

Import substitutes are also expressed as a fraction of total output

$$M_s = m_2 (Y_n), \qquad (10d)$$

and the import-substitution coefficient (m_2) is variable.

By substituting the M_p and M_s equations into M*
equation (10b), the import function becomes

$$M^* = m_1 (Y_n) - m_2 (Y_n) = (m_1 - m_2) Y_n \qquad (10e)$$

or substituting for Y_n and using the target growth
rate

$$M^* = (m_1 - m_2) Y_o (1 + r)^n. \qquad (10f)$$

Import functions used by others are rather different. Avramovic, for instance, considers imports
as a residual value by adding the internal gap and
exports together. Vanek again disaggregates total
imports into a number of components such as raw materials (M_r), fuels (M_f), machinery (M_m), and transportation equipment (M_t). These components are in

turn related to GNP or values added by sectors,
$M_r = 0.062 \ V_{3,4}$.[23]

An export function is somewhat different from
the import function stated above. Most external-gap
models treat exports as an exogenous variable, and
they are assumed to grow at a constant rate annually.[24]

$$X_n = X_O \ (1 + x)^n \qquad\qquad (11)$$

where X_O and x stand for exports of goods and services
in the base year and the growth rate of exports, respectively. This procedure is also followed in this
study, owing to the virtual impossibility of obtain-
ing a precise functional relationship with such factors as those for the investment, saving, and import
functions. Exports depend heavily on foreign demand.
Not only does demand for a single developing country's
exports depend on incomes and a score of influential
policy factors in advanced countries, but this demand
is also heavily affected by export supplies in other
developing countries. Therefore, it is extremely
difficult to project exports of a developing country
whose exports represent a small fraction of total
world exports.

In contrast to our export function, Vanek again
uses a sectoral model for exports. According to
Vanek, a number of export components are related to
growth rates of these components, determined by the
terms of trade or by other independent variables.[25]

So far the import and export functions have been
discussed separately. Substituting the two functions
in equations (10f) and (11) into equations (2) to obtain the final form of external gap, we obtain

$$FK = (m_1 - m_2) \ Y_O \ (1 + r)^n - X_O \ (1 + x)^n. \qquad (12)$$

As noted before, the import function of the
external-gap theory is based on the notion that a
minimum of imports is required to reach the target
level of total output. This normative notion is very
different from, if not flatly opposed to, the positive

theory of free trade. The classical free-trade principle generally postulates that imports are made if
they are relatively more advantageous in terms of
real-commodity prices and underlying factor costs
than commodities produced domestically. Under this
principle--translated into money terms and at a
fixed-exchange rate--imports will increase and decrease automatically as domestic and foreign national
prices or incomes increase and decrease.[26] The import function in this study recognizes that the minimum level of imports to reach the target-output
level may be different from the imports that would
occur by applying this principle.

Linder, who advocates the use of the concept of
minimum imports required for growth, argues that conventional free-trade theory is inadequate and inappli-
cable in analyzing the effects on developing countries
of trade with advanced countries, because "its analytical apparatus is geared solely to the question of
the welfare and structural effects of the realloca-
tion of given, fully utilized resources resulting
from changes in relative prices in connection with
trade."[27] The conventional theory is primarily concerned with the optimum allocation of resources in a
static sense. There is no room for unutilized resources under this theory. In this study, however,
required imports are defined as those that will put
unutilized and underutilized resources, particularly
labor, into total potential output Y, and a trade
deficit resulting from this objective is accepted as
the external gap. This concept is called the "lever-
age effect," without which resources remain unutilized.[28] A developing country must import certain
goods, such as raw materials and capital goods, in
order to realize growth.[29] Furthermore, a developing
country needs "new inventive technology to stimulate
existing simple techniques."[30] Imports demanded in
developing countries are usually larger than potential exports.

Nevertheless, one typical assumption of development models is that exports are assumed to increase
over time. Perhaps one reason for this optimistic
assumption is that exports might serve as "the engine

of the economic growth" in developing countries.[31]
Nurske is among the few writers who give a pessimistic picture of export prospects in underdeveloped
countries.[32] He argues that there is an "export
lag"[33] in less-developed countries (LDC's). Histori-
cally, exports of industrial countries have increased
more than those of less-developed countries.

In the case of Korea, the prospects may not be
gloomy. The growth of exports of all underdeveloped
countries as a group may be limited by international-
demand conditions, which have been influenced in part
by the introduction of synthetic raw materials. Demand is important, and hence export prospects for an
individual country may be different, especially as
export diversification progresses, from the outlook
for developing countries as a whole. Some countries
--such as Taiwan, India, the Philippines, Israel, and
Mexico--have succeeded moderately in recent years in
expanding their exports of light manufactured goods
on the basis of internal transformation. The projection of an export growth rate for Korea should not
be based on international-demand conditions for primary goods alone.

International-demand developments and not necessarily current comparative costs should be considered
in determining the most advantageous form of Korean
export growth. Classical theory suggests that developing countries might best produce relatively labor-
intensive primary goods. However, this appraisal is
open to attack since growth changes comparative advantage, and change takes place in both developed and
developing countries. Korea may become an exporter
of manufactured goods as the country diversifies its
internal economy and may thus participate in the rapid
growth of import demands for manufactured goods among
industrialized countries.[34]

THE PROBLEM OF DEBT SERVICE AND GROSS BORROWING

As stated previously, gross external capital
needs (EK) are the sum of foreign capital needs (FK),
debt service (DS), and the change in foreign reserve,

d(Fx). FK is either the internal gap or the external
gap. FK in the nth year is in fact the net-capital
inflow and is composed of transfer payments (T), direct investment (DI), and net borrowing (D). (In
contrast to our model, Vanek assumes there will be
no capital flow of other than public and publicly
guaranteed debts in the future.)

$$FK_n = T_n + DI_n + D_n \tag{13a}$$

Debt service (DS) in the nth year can also be
broken down into the following components,

$$DS_n = (DS_p)_n + (i_s)_n + (A_s)_n \tag{13b}$$

where $(DS)_p$ stands for debt service on past debts,
i_s for the average interest payments on subsequent
debts, and A_s for the average amortization payments
on subsequent debts.

Actually, D is net borrowing excluding debt service plus the change in reserves, and new gross borrowing (GD) is D + DS + d (Fx). Debt service on past
debts is given from data on interest and amortization
schedules. Interest on subsequent debts (i_s) in the
nth year is the average interest on cumulative outstanding debts (COD) accumulated until the (n-1)th
year.

$$(i_s) = i(COD)_{n-1} = i\ (AOD_{n-1} + AOD_{n-2} + \cdots + AOD_o)$$

$$= i \sum_{n=o}^{n-1} AOD_n \tag{13c}$$

where AOD is annual increase in outstanding debt
which excludes amortization payment on subsequent
debts. Amortization is calculated by using the average maturity period of debts (t) and allowing for the
average grace period (g).

$$(A_s)_n = \frac{1}{t}\ (GD)_{n-g-1} + \frac{1}{t}\ (GD)_{n-g-2} + \cdots + \frac{1}{t}\ (GD)_{n-g}$$

$$= \sum_{n-1}^{m-g} \frac{1}{t}\ GD_n \tag{13d}$$

In the (A_s) equation, the zero year is not the base
year but the year when the grace period ends. The
level of foreign reserve is related to imports of
goods and services.[35]

$$FX_n = f(M)_n \qquad\qquad (14)$$

It is generally agreed that international reserves must grow along with trade through time not
only in developed but also in underdeveloped countries. Higher reserves are needed by LDC's, with
more volatile levels of exports and capital imports,
than by the richer and more diversified economies of
the advanced countries. Furthermore, the more adequate amount of liquidity is needed in LDC's to permit financing of short-run deficits reflecting purely
temporary fluctuations in foreign-exchange expenditures in current and capital accounts.

The problem is now to select a correct value of
FK, depending on whether the ex ante internal or external gap is chosen. Only one value--whichever is
the larger of the two--is selected for FK in this
study. Stated differently, the capital inflow must
cover the larger of the two gaps.[36] Selection of the
smaller gap will limit the growth potential of a
country. The larger gap "controls the rate of growth
of GNP and the inflow of capital."[37]

A case in point: If domestic savings are large
enough for ex ante savings to equal ex ante investment, there may still be an external gap if the
minimum-import requirement is greater than potential
exports. The minimum needs of foreign capital, therefore, are equivalent to the larger gap.

After the larger gap is selected, the smaller of
the ex ante gaps is adjusted to the ex post equality.
The adjustment process toward the larger gap is described by Chenery and Strout as follows:

> When the capital inflow determined by the
> savings-investment gap in equation (2) is
> greater than the minimum trade gap, the
> two gaps can be equated by having imports

> in excess of the specified minimum or
> exports less than the assumed maximum
> of equation (14). When the minimum
> trade gap is larger . . . either saving
> will fall below the saving potential
> specified by equation (5) or less produc-
> tive investment will take place.[38]

According to Vanek, policy measures can help in
the adjustment of the two gaps. Vanek calls the
larger gap "the minimum consistent foreign resource
requirements."[39] He prefers policy measures to auton-
omous economic adjustment, for free-market forces do
not always work properly in developing countries.
Consequently, when the external gap is larger, the
appropriate course of action would be to reduce savings or to stimulate investment through tax changes
or other policy measures.

SUMMARY

The theory offered in this study is designed to
be more sophisticated than other theories. Rosenstein-
Rodan and Fei and Paauw use the internal gap--which
is the difference between total investment requirements and domestic savings--as an estimate for
foreign-capital needs. But they ignore the external
gap, which is the difference between total import requirements and export earnings. Chenery and Strout
deal with the two gaps, and yet they neglect to account for the problem of debt service in a borrowing
country. Although Avramovic and Vanek deal with the
problem of debt service, Avramovic ignores the import
function, and Vanek assumes no foreign-capital inflow
other than external debt. Our model takes into consideration both the importance of two-gap analysis
and of the debt service arising not only from future
external debts but also past debts.

The theory of external-capital needs can be summarized in the following equation forms:

Variables

FK	Foreign-capital needs
EK	External-capital needs
Y	Gross national product (GNP)
Y*	Target GNP
I_r	Required investment
S_d	Domestic savings
M_r	Required imports
M_p	Potential imports
M_s	Import substitutes
X	Exports
T	Transfer payments
DI	Foreign direct investment
D	Net external borrowing
OD	Outstanding external debts
DS	Debt service
DS_p	Debt on past debts
A_s	Amortization payments on subsequent debts
FX	Foreign-exchange reserve

Parameters

r	Target growth rate of GNP
k	Incremental capital-output ratio
s	Average-savings rate
s'	Marginal-savings rate
m_1	Potential import-GNP ratio
m_2	Import-substitution coefficient
x	Export growth rate
i_s	Interest on subsequent debts
n	Year
t	Maturity period on external debts
g	Grace period
f	Ratio of foreign-exchange reserve to imports

Internal gap

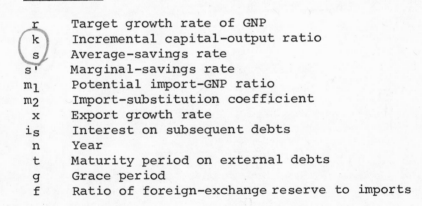

$$FK = I_r - S_d \qquad (1)$$

$$FK = \left[kr\,(Y_0)\,(1+r)^n \right]$$
$$-\left[s\,(Y_0 + \sum_{n=1}^{n} s'\,\left\{ Y_0\,(1+r)^n \right. \right.$$
$$\left. \left. - Y_0\,(1+r)^{n-1} \right\} \right] \qquad (9)$$

External gap

$$FK = M_r - X \tag{2}$$

$$FK = \left[(m_1 - m_2) \left\{ Y_0 (1 + r)^n \right\} \right]$$
$$- \left[X_0 (1 + x)_n \right] \tag{12}$$

External capital needs

$$EK = FK + DS + d \ (FX) \tag{3}$$

Ex post identity

$$Y = C + I + (X - M) \tag{4a}$$

$$I - S_d = M - X \tag{4b}$$

Target growth of GNP

$$(Y^*)_n = Y_0 (1 + r)^n \tag{5}$$

Investment function

$$I_r = kr (Y^*) \tag{6a}$$

Incremental capital-output ratio

$$k = \frac{dK}{dY} = \frac{I}{dY} \tag{7a}$$

$$k_n = \frac{I_n}{Y_n - Y_{n-1}} \tag{7b}$$

$$\bar{k} = \frac{1}{n} (k_1 + k_2 + \ldots + k_n) \tag{7c}$$

Savings function

$$S_n = s \ (Y_0) + \sum_{n=1}^{n} \left[Y_0 (1 + r)^n \right.$$
$$\left. - Y_0 (1 + r)^{n-1} \right] \tag{8}$$

Import function

$$M^* = m\,(Y_n) \tag{10a}$$

$$M^* = M_p - M_s \tag{10b}$$

$$M_p = m_1\,(Y_n) \tag{10c}$$

$$M_s = m_2\,(Y_n) \tag{10d}$$

$$M^* = (m_1 - m_2)\,Y_n \tag{10e}$$

$$M^* = (m_1 - m_2)\,Y_o\,(1 + r)^n \tag{10f}$$

Export function

$$X_n = X_o\,(1 + x)^n \tag{11}$$

External debts and debt service

$$FK_n = T_n + DI_n + D_n \tag{13a}$$

$$DS_n = (DS_p)_n + (i_s)_n + (A_s)_n \tag{13b}$$

$$(i_s)_n = i\,(COD)_{n-1} = i\,(AOD_{n-1} + \ldots + AOD_o) = i \sum_{n=o}^{n-1} AOD_n \tag{13c}$$

$$(A_s)_n = \frac{1}{t}\,(GD)_{n-g-1}$$

$$+ \ldots + \frac{1}{t}\,(GD)_{n-g}$$

$$= \sum_{n=1}^{m-g} \frac{1}{t}\,GD_n \tag{13d}$$

$$FK_n = f\,(M)_n \tag{14}$$

NOTES

1. The contributions referred to are the following: P. N. Rosenstein-Rodan, "International Aid for Underdeveloped Countries," The Review of Economics and Statistics (May, 1961), pp. 107-38; John C. H. Fei and Douglas S. Paauw, "Foreign Assistance and Self-Help: A Reappraisal of Development Finance," The Review of Economics and Statistics (August, 1965), pp. 251-67; D. Avramovic, Economic Growth and External Debt (Baltimore: Johns Hopkins Press, 1964); Hollis B. Chenery and A. M. Strout, "Foreign Assistance and Economic Development," The American Economic Review (September, 1966), pp. 679-733; Jaroslav Vanek (with the assistance of Richard Billsborrow), Estimating Foreign Resource Needs for Economic Development (New York: McGraw-Hill, 1967); R. I. McKinnon, "Foreign Exchange Constraints in Economic Development and Efficient Aid Allocation," The Economic Journal (June, 1964), pp. 388-409; S. R. Merret and J. S. Wabe, "A Modification of the Savings-Investment Approach to Devaluation," Oxford Economic Papers (November, 1964), pp. 418-22; and A. D. Krueger, "Balance of Payments Theory," Journal of Economic Literature (March, 1969), pp. 1-26.

2. See Charles P. Kindleberger, International Economics (Homewood, Ill.: Richard D. Irwin, Inc., 1963), especially Chapter 10, for a thorough discussion of the ex post identity between internal and external gaps.

3. Chenery and Strout, op. cit., p. 684.

4. Avramovic, op. cit., pp. 156-57.

5. Vanek, op. cit., pp. 11-12.

6. R. F. Harrod, Towards a Dynamic Economics (London: Macmillan & Co., 1963), pp. 81-82; and Evsey D. Domar, Essays in the Theory of Economic Growth (New York: Oxford University Press, 1957), pp. 91-95.

7. Rosenstein-Rodan, op. cit., pp. 117-35; Avramovic, op. cit., pp. 156-57; Chenery and Strout, op. cit., p. 685.

8. Rosenstein-Rodan, op. cit., p. 117.

9. Ibid., p. 117; Fei and Paauw, op. cit., pp. 254-62.

10. Solomon Fabricant, Basic Facts on Productivity Change, Occasional Paper 63, National Bureau of Economic Research, Inc., pp. 18-19; Harvey Leibenstein, "The Incremental Capital-Output Ratio," Review of Economics and Statistics (February, 1966), pp. 20-25; Surendra J. Patel, "A Note on the Incremental Capital-Output Ratio and Economic Growth in Developing Countries," Kyklos, XXI (1968).

11. Vanek, op. cit., pp. 125-26.

12. Ibid.

13. Chenery and Strout, op. cit., pp. 685-705.

14. Fei and Paauw, op. cit., p. 252.

15. Vanek, op. cit., p. 32.

16. Ibid., pp. 33-34.

17. Hollis B. Chenery, "Patterns of Industrial Growth," The American Economic Review (September, 1960), pp. 624-25.

18. Avramovic, op. cit., pp. 47-49.

19. Ibid., p. 48.

20. See Chenery and Strout, op. cit., pp. 688-91; Vanek, op. cit., pp. 105-11.

21. Chenery and Strout, op. cit., p. 689.

22. Staffan Burenstam Linder, Trade and Trade Policy for Development (New York: Frederick A. Praeger, 1967), pp. 20-21.

23. Vanek, op. cit., pp. 43-47.

24. Chenery and Strout, op. cit., p. 690.

25. Vanek, op. cit., pp. 41-43.

26. The modern free-trade theory is discussed in G. Haberler, The Theory of International Trade (New York: Macmillan, 1963; also see Jacob Viner, Studies in The Theory of International Trade (New York: reprinted by Augustus M. Kelley, Publisher, 1965).

27. Linder, op. cit., p. 2.

28. Ibid., pp. 2-3; also see H. Myint, "The Classical Theory of International Trade and Underdeveloped Countries," Economic Journal (June, 1958), pp. 317-37.

29. Linder, op. cit., pp. 11-12.

30. Ibid., p. 15.

31. W. Arthur Lewis, Development Planning (New York: Harper & Row, 1966), pp. 38-40.

32. A pessimistic view by other writers such as R. Prebisch, H. W. Singer, and D. Seers is discussed in Chapter 3.

33. Ragner Nurske, Equilibrium and Growth in the World Economy (Cambridge: Harvard University Press, 1961, pp. 245-47 and 278.

34. See S. B. Linder, An Essay on Trade and Transformation (New York: John Wiley, 1961), Chapter 3; and Linder, Trade and Trade Policy, op. cit., pp. 36-37.

35. See P. B. Kenen and E. B. Yudin, "The Demand for International Reserves," The Review of Economics and Statistics (August, 1965), pp. 242-50; Robert Triffin, Gold and the Dollar Crisis (New Haven: Yale University Press, 1961(, pp. 35-36.

36. See Chenery and Strout, op. cit., p. 690; Vanek, op. cit., pp. 106-8.

37. Chenery and Strout, op. cit., p. 690.

38. Ibid.

39. Vanek, op. cit., p. 107.

CHAPTER **2** ESTIMATING EXTERNAL-
CAPITAL NEEDS

INTRODUCTION

Based on the theoretical framework discussed in
Chapter 1, future external-capital needs of Korea
are estimated in this chapter. The objective is not
to attempt to predict precisely the future behavior
of the economy, but to obtain a rough indication of
how much foreign capital would be necessary for all
purposes, including debt service. Also, the objective is to identify what factors vitally affect the
amount of foreign-capital needs and the forces which
determine the parameter values and the sensitivity
of external capital. This will, in turn, suggest
what areas may be susceptible to policy intervention
and indicate what kinds of policy forces and direc-
tions should be followed to ensure development.

The intentional policy-oriented estimation is
strongly motivated by the belief that it is possible
to improve Korea's growth rate and to achieve other
economic objectives. Long-term economic projections
by the United Nations Economic Commission for Asia
and the Far East (ECAFE) are also essentially intentional or purposive projections rather than extrapola-
tions based solely on past parameters.[1] In Korea, as
in many developing countries, the main objectives are:

1. To achieve a self-sufficient economy
    independent of foreign aid,

2. To increase the level and growth rate of
    national income,[2]

3. To bring about balance-of-payments equili-
    brium. (Balance-of-payments equilibrium is

25

defined for this purpose as equivalent to
current-account balance in the absence of
trade and exchange restrictions.)

In "gap" terminology, the basic objective is to close
the internal gap as well as external gap along with
the achievement of an assumed-target GNP, which will
also reduce the burden of external-debt service.

Aside from an intentional projection, the precise prediction of external-capital needs is almost
impossible in the case of Korea. Future parameters
may not necessarily follow the past trend values,
mainly because in pursuit of the desired objectives
certain parameters are to be adjusted by new policy
measures, and the existing parameters are "subject
to the unpredictable variations in time and space."[3]
For instance, a devaluation or a political change may
affect all the parameters systematically.

Furthermore, only the general magnitude rather
than a precise quantification of external-capital
needs is attempted because of the poor quality of the
available data. Neither are detailed figures available, nor are the available data very reliable. For
example, GNP figures are inaccurate owing to changing
systems of compiling over time and meager records on
the part of government, business, and individuals,
including most farmers. Therefore, the interpreta-
tion of the data is difficult.

Another and related purpose of the estimate is
to deal with the question of whether capital-exporting
countries have an incentive to invest in Korea. There
is an analogy with a corporate borrower who estimates
the profitability of an investment project. The project will be carried out if the rate of return is higher than the cost of capital, if a part of earnings is
saved and invested, and if earnings are expected to
grow consistently in the future. Likewise, foreigners,
both private and public investors, will be interested
in the "strengthening of the borrowing economy."[4]

An estimate of external-capital needs of a country should show explicitly or implicitly whether total
output grows consistently, whether the marginal-savings

rate and the export growth rate are high enough to
finance the bulk of investment and import requirements domestically, and whether a country is able to
service external debt.[5] In the process of estimating
capital needs, the debt-servicing capacity of Korea
will play a major part. No lending country will supply the full amount of external-capital requirements
estimated on the basis of gap theories simply because
these countries are underdeveloped.

Pincus, however, doubts the usefulness of calculating foreign-capital requirements based on the
internal- and external-gap theories. He claims that
there is no general and objective way to determine
the appropriate amount of foreign capital that should
be transferred from the rich to the poor countries.[6]
Hence, he believes that the ultimate criterion for
actual capital transfer to developing countries depends on how much the rich countries will offer. The
major, underlying issue in capital transfer, according to Pincus, is "ethical."[7]

The role of an ethical criterion is, however,
open to challenge. Perhaps economic interest is more
important than ethical interest affecting capital
movements. It is reasonable to assume that foreign
capital in significant amounts may actually flow into Korea, if the motivation behind the capital movements is compatible with the mutual interests of advanced countries and Korea. The future prospects
for foreign-capital inflow will be favorable if the
past performance in economic progress and political
stability is on the "plus" side.

Furthermore, the very exercise of estimation and
the attempt to derive realistic parameter values
yield considerable insight into how and by what means
policy adjustments may be made to remove the needs for
foreign capital or to insulate the domestic, economic
performance from fluctuations in it. By varying the
critical values of targets based on the sensitivity
analysis, we can foresee a possible outcome of alternative developments, and alternative policy objectives
are derived. Consequently, the estimation on the
basis of analytical framework is superior to an arbitrary method.

HISTORICAL PERFORMANCE OF INTERNAL AND
EXTERNAL GAP

The ex post internal and external gaps have been relatively large in Korea because excess investment and imports have been permitted by a sizable flow of foreign resources.

The Internal Gap

The internal gap in Table 2.1 shows gross investment, domestic savings, and foreign savings in Korea from 1954 through 1968. It has been difficult so far in Korea to finance the investment necessary for economic development through domestic savings. Less than one third of gross investment has been financed by domestic savings over the period 1955-68 as a whole. But the general trend of self-financing has been upward. The average share of domestic savings as a percentage of total investment increased from 22.8 percent in 1954-56 to 46.7 percent in 1962-66, and to 52.8 percent in 1967-68. The upward trend became more rapid after 1963, following the initiation of the First Five-Year Economic Plan, rising to a peak of 57.6 percent in 1967. Nevertheless, even in that year almost one half of investment was still financed from foreign resources.

The External Gap

The main feature of Korea's balance of payments has been the wide gap between imports and exports of goods and services as shown in Table 2.2. Korea had an average annual-import surplus of $308 million during the 1954-68 period. Again the general trend of import surplus in relative terms has been downward since 1954. The import surplus, or net inflow of foreign aid and capital, as a percentage of total imports, has declined from 81.4 percent in 1954-56 to 52.2 percent in 1962-66 and to 40.4 percent in 1967-68. This of course implies that the share of imports financed through exports has increased during the 1954-68 period.

The import surplus in absolute terms also declined after 1957 when imports financed by foreign

TABLE 2.1

Investment, Domestic Savings, and Foreign Savings
(in billions of Korean won)

Year	Gross Investment Amount	Domestic Savings[a] Amount	Percent of Gross Investment	Foreign Savings[b] (net capital inflow) Amount	Percent of Gross Investment
1954	7.78	3.26	41.8	4.52	58.2
1955	13.81	5.68	41.1	8.13	58.9
1956	14.41	2.07	-14.4	16.48	114.4
1957	30.26	10.93	36.2	19.33	63.8
1958	26.73	10.27	38.4	16.46	61.6
1959	23.72	8.66	36.5	15.06	63.5
1960	26.80	3.79	14.5	22.91	85.5
1961	38.79	11.32	29.2	27.41	70.8
1962	45.57	5.17	11.4	40.25	88.6
1963	89.68	33.68	37.5	56.01	62.5
1964	101.24	48.38	48.3	52.36	51.7
1965	118.48	60.75	51.3	57.73	48.7
1966	223.11	121.32	54.4	101.19	45.6
1967	272.20	156.79	57.6	115.41	42.4
1968	421.31	235.93	56.0	185.38	44.0
Averages					
1954–56	13.0	2.29	22.8	9.71	77.2
1957–61	29.3	9.0	30.7	20.3	69.3
1962–66	115.6	54.0	46.7	61.6	53.3
1967–68	346.8	196.36	56.8	150.4	43.2

[a]Domestic savings are gross savings (including depreciation) and include statistical discrepancies.

[b]Foreign savings are the difference between gross investment and domestic savings and include statistical discrepancies.

Sources: Calculations from data in Economic Statistics Yearbook (The Bank of Korea, 1965, 1966, and 1967; The Monthly Statistical Review (The Bank of Korea, July, 1967); Monthly Economic Statistics (The Bank of Korea, November, 1969).

29

TABLE 2.2

Imports, Exports, and Import Surplus
(in millions of U.S. dollars)

	Imports[a]	Exports		Import Surplus	
Year	Amount	Amount	Percent of Imports	Amount	Percent of Imports
1954	244.6	54.5	22.3	-180.1	77.7
1955	377.2	71.3	21.1	-265.9	78.9
1956	393.9	63.0	16.0	-330.9	84.0
1957	466.2	78.7	16.9	-387.5	83.1
1958	403.6	92.4	22.9	-311.2	77.1
1959	331.1	103.6	31.3	-227.5	68.7
1960	378.8	116.9	30.9	-261.9	69.1
1961	343.0	145.6	42.3	-198.4	57.7
1962	452.1	163.2	36.1	-288.9	63.9
1963	574.8	175.5	30.5	-399.3	69.5
1964	419.6	211.0	50.3	-208.6	49.7
1965	486.9	289.8	59.9	-197.1	40.1
1966	771.7	454.7	59.0	-317.0	41.0
1967	1,043.9	642.9	61.5	-401.0	38.5
1968	1,525.4	880.3	57.7	-645.1	42.3

Averages

1954-56	338.6	62.9	18.6	-259.0	81.4
1957-61	384.5	107.4	27.9	-277.3	72.1
1962-66	541.0	258.8	47.8	-282.2	52.2
1967-68	1,284.6	761.6	59.6	-523.0	40.4

[a]Import of goods and services exclude interest on
external debts after 1962. Average annual interest
payments were negligible from 1954 through 1961 because the bulk of foreign loans occurred after 1962.

Sources: Calculations from data in Economic Statistics Yearbook (The Bank of Korea, 1959,
1961, and 1967; Monthly Economic Statistics
(The Bank of Korea, November, 1969).

aid reached their peak, or from $387.5 million in
1957 to $198.4 million in 1961, and total imports
actually declined in 1957-59. Imports started to
increase again significantly during the first-plan
period (1962-66), because the plan required large
imports of heavy-investment goods and raw materials.
Foreign loans helped finance the increase in imports.[8]
The ratio of the import surplus to total imports also rose again, from 37.7 percent in 1961 to 63.9
percent in 1962 and 69.5 percent in 1963. In the
most recent years, however, exports have increased
more rapidly as the fruits of import substitution
have begun to materialize. Thus, the ratio of the
import surplus to total imports has shown a downward
trend (49.7 percent in 1964, 41 percent in 1966, and
40.4 percent in 1967-68).

RAPID ECONOMIC GROWTH

The improvement in the internal as well as the
external gap has been both cause and effect of consistent economic growth in Korea. The increase in
investments and exports contributed to rapid economic growth, and rapid growth in turn brought about a
high savings rate and large import requirements.
Rapid economic growth is clearly reflected in GNP
growth rates, per-capita income, and industrial production.

GNP Growth Rate

Since the signing of the truce agreement in
1953, the gross national product has increased consistently. As noted, this growth has been made possible by foreign capital, although domestic savings
have started to play an important role in recent
years.

During 1954-56, the average growth rate of GNP
in real terms averaged 4.5 percent annually, as shown
in Table 2.3. This growth was made possible because
of reconstruction aid from the United States and because of good harvests in 1954 and 1955. But the
growth rate dropped to 1.2 percent in 1956 because of

TABLE 2.3

Gross National Product and Its Growth Rate[a]
(in billions of won)

| Year | At Current Prices | | At 1965 Constant Prices | | Percent of Wholesale Price Change |
	Amount	Year-to-Year Change	Amount	Year-to-Year Change	
1953	48.18	--	421.93	--	--
1954	66.88	38.8	447.36	6.0	28.3
1955	116.06	73.5	474.54	6.1	80.9
1956	152.44	31.3	480.47	1.2	31.7
1957	197.78	29.7	522.73	8.8	16.2
1958	207.19	4.8	551.69	5.5	-6.3
1959	221.00	6.7	575.84	4.4	2.4
1960	246.69	11.6	589.07	2.3	10.7
1961	296.82	20.3	613.61	4.2	13.2
1962	348.58	17.4	634.97	3.5	9.4
1963	487.96	40.0	693.03	9.1	20.6
1964	696.79	42.8	750.31	8.3	34.7
1965	805.85	15.7	805.85	7.4	10.0
1966	1,032.04	28.1	913.82	13.4	7.6
1967	1,242.35	20.4	995.16	8.9	6.8
1968	1,575.65	26.8	1,127.32	13.2	8.1
Averages					
1954-56	111.8	47.9	467.5	4.5	47.0
1957-61	233.9	14.6	570.6	5.0	7.2
1962-66	614.2	28.8	759.6	8.3	16.5
1954-66	375.1	27.7	619.5	6.2	21.6
1967-68	1,409.0	23.6	1,061.2	11.1	7.5

[a] The national income accounts were revised in 1967.
There is a great discrepancy between the 1967 revision and previous national income accounts.

Source: Calculations from data in The Monthly Statistical Review (The Bank of Korea, July, 1967);
Monthly Economic Statistics (The Bank of Korea, November, 1969).

a crop failure. At the same time, this period was
characterized by sharp inflation--the average GNP
growth rate at current market prices was 47.9 percent.

As financial stabilization programs were carried
out in 1957-59, inflationary pressures slowed down
substantially. (Stabilization programs will be discussed further in Chapter 5.) The average price increase was 7.2 percent per annum in 1957-61 as against
47 percent in 1954-56. The stabilization programs
reduced the growth of the money supply and of aggregate demand. Also, foreign aid started to decline
after 1957. As a result, the real GNP growth rate
reached 8.8 percent in 1957, and then it declined to
5.5 percent in 1958 and 4.4 percent in 1959. The
rate again dropped in 1960, to 2.3 percent, when the
student uprising ousted President Syngman Rhee and
the economy was paralyzed. The over-all average
growth rate amounted to 5 percent annually in 1957-61.

The military revolution of 1961 brought about
not only political and social changes but also marked
the turning point in economic growth. Except for a
year of a partial crop failure--1962--the real GNP
growth rate averaged more than 9 percent, and the
average growth rate was 8.3 percent per annum during
the first economic-plan period (1962-66) and 11.1
percent per annum in 1967-68. This rapid growth was
possible because of increased investment with the
help of foreign loans, and because of vital economic
reforms relating to the exchange rate, interest rates,
and taxation.[9] Inflation recurred again as a result
of growth-oriented policies in the early part of the
plan but slowed down in the latter part.

The average growth rate of 8.3 percent in 1962-
66 is higher than many advanced as well as developing
countries, as shown in Table 2.4. It is understandable that many mature industrial countries such as
the United States (5.8 percent), West Germany (2.5
percent), Japan (9.3 percent), and the United Kingdom
(0.5 percent) would have a lower average growth rate.
But the Korean growth rate, especially in 1966, is
much higher than that of many developing countries

TABLE 2.4

Economic Growth Rates of Selected Countries
(in percentages)

Country	Base	1962-66 Average	1966
Korea	GNP (1965)	8.3	13.4
United States	GNP (1958)	5.6	5.8
Canada	GDP (1957)	6.2	6.0
Mexico	GNP (1950)	6.5	6.5
England	GDP (1958)	2.6	0.5
West Germany	GDP (1954)	4.3	2.5
France	GDP (1959)	5.0	4.5
Italy	GDP (1958)	4.5	5.0
Japan	GNP (1960)	8.1	9.3
Taiwan	GDP (1952)	8.5	8.0
Philippines	GDP (1955)	4.6	5.4
Thailand	GDP (1962)	7.7	6.5
Malaysia	GDP (1959)	6.3	6.7
India	GDP (1948)	2.9	3.9

Sources: Yearbook of National Accounts Statistics,
United Nations, 1966; Monthly Bulletin of
Statistics, United Nations (December, 1967);
Economic Report of the President (U.S.
Government Printing Office, 1968); Economist
December 31, 1966; Seoul Kyungje Shinmoon
(Seoul daily economic newspaper; Seoul,
January 29, 1967).

which are in the early stages of development, such
as Taiwan (8.0 percent), Mexico (6.5 percent), the
Philippines (5.4 percent), Thailand (6.5 percent),
and India (3.9 percent).

Per-Capita Income

In the seven-year period ended 1968, the most
rapid growth rate of GNP in Korean economic history
was recorded. In a stricter sense, economic growth
should be measured by per-capita income, because per-
capita income is a good index of economic growth. [10]
The ultimate economic objective is not a high growth
rate of GNP as such, but rather a high standard of
living and the welfare of the individual. If the
population growth rate exceeds the GNP growth rate,
per-capita income will decline. Furthermore, a population explosion may reduce savings and capital
formation and thereby frustrate the growth process.

As can be seen from Table 2.5, per-capita income has increased consistently as a result of high
GNP growth rates and a slow rate of population increase. Real GNP at 1965 prices increased by 137.2
percent between 1954 and 1968, while per-capita GNP
increased by 72.2 percent and population increased
by 46.3 percent in the same period. The growth rate
of real GNP averaged 6.8 percent per annum, while
that of per-capita GNP averaged 3.6 percent per annum. Average per-capita GNP in Korean won increased
by 5.4 percent per annum in 1962-66 and by 8 percent
per annum in 1967-68.

Although both total output and per-capita income have increased at a rapid rate in recent years,
the per-capita income of Korea is still one of the
lowest in the world. Table 2.6 shows per-capita incomes for various countries. Korea had a per-capita
income of $101.00 in 1965 and ranked very low, which
shows the importance of further growth.

Industrial Production and Structure

The consistent economic growth from 1954 through
1968 has been led by spectacular growth in industrial

TABLE 2.5

Per-Capita Gross National Product
and National Income

Year	(1)[a] GNP	NI	(2)[b] Population	(3)[c] Per-Capita GNP	NI	(4)[d] Per-Capita GNP
1954	66.88	60.12	20,823	3,212	2,887	21,484
1955	116.68	106.12	21,424	5,446	4,953	22,146
1956	152.44	139.76	22,042	6,916	6,341	22,478
1957	197.78	179.65	22,677	8,772	7,922	23,051
1958	207.76	184.86	23,331	8,880	7,923	23,696
1959	221.00	193.36	24,003	9,207	8,056	23,990
1960	246.69	215.89	24,695	9,989	8,742	23,858
1961	296.82	264.64	25,402	11,685	10,418	24,156
1962	348.58	303.27	26,125	13,343	11,608	24,305
1963	487.96	431.57	26,868	18,161	16,063	25,794
1964	696.79	627.00	27,631	25,218	22,692	27,155
1965	805.85	713.06	28,377	28,398	25,128	28,398
1966	1,032.04	901.86	29,086	35,482	31,007	31,418
1967	1,242.35	1,069.90	29,784	41,711	35,890	33,412
1968	1,575.65	1,328.70	30,469	51,713	43,608	36,998

Annual Average Percentage Increase

1955–56	52.4	54.1	2.9	48.3	49.8	2.3
1957–61	14.6	14.1	2.9	11.4	8.6	1.2
1962–66	28.8	28.5	2.7	25.2	25.0	5.4
1954–66	26.7	26.7	2.8	23.3	23.3	3.2
1967–68	23.6	23.1	2.4	20.7	18.6	8.0

[a]Column (1) is in terms of billions of won at current prices.
[b]Column (2) is population in thousands.
[c]Column (3) is per-capita income in won at current prices.
[d]Column (4) is per-capita GNP at 1965 constant prices in won.

Source: Economic Statistics Yearbook (The Bank of Korea, 1967, 1968, 1969).

36

TABLE 2.6

Per-Capita National Income of Selected Countries
(in U.S. dollars)

Country	1958	1963	1964	1965
United States	2,115	2,562	2,713	2,893
Canada	1,503	1,602	1,696	1,825
Australia	1,126	1,483	1,590	1,620
England	1,005	1,287	1,374	1,451
West Germany	838	1,254	1,357	1,447
France	1,003	1,270	1,370	1,436
Japan	284	559	630	696
Mexico	272	349	394	412
Colombia	188	223	235	237
Malaysia	194	224	234	250
Philippines	187	209	213	219
Taiwan	124	151	175	185
Thailand	80	98	102	105
Korea	78	87	95	101
India	64	78	88	86
Burma	53	61	56	--

Note: For most of the countries represented, the
estimates have been prepared by converting
the official national income figures by the
prevailing dollar exchange rates which are
normally the par value of the currency. For
Korea, which does not have the par value, the
exchange parity rates estimated by the Bank
of Korea are used. Caution needs to be exer-
cised in the use of estimates, because the
average relationship of the internal purchasing powers of currencies is rarely the prevailing exchange rate.

Source: Yearbook of National Accounts Statistics,
United Nations (1966), pp. 730-33.

production. During the 1954-68 period, secondary
industry has increased at 15 percent per annum compared to a 4.5 percent growth rate for primary industry and 5.6 percent in the case of tertiary industry. (The industry groupings are defined so as to
be inclusive of total GNP.)

These divergent growth rates of industrial
groups are reflected in a change in the industrial
structure of the economy. The relative size of primary industry as a percentage of total industrial
output has declined sharply while tertiary industry
has stayed comparatively stable, as shown in Table
2.7 Between 1954 and 1968, the relative share of
GNP originating in primary industry has declined from
42 percent to 28.9 percent, while the share of secondary industry has risen from 13 percent to 34 percent. Meanwhile, the share of tertiary industry has
declined slightly, from 44.6 percent in 1954 to 37.2
percent in 1968.

The change in the Korean industrial structure
conforms to Clark's hypothesis. He postulates that
the relative shares of secondary and tertiary industries rise in the course of economic development.[11]
The hypothesis is also supported by Kuznets who shows
marked shifts in the shares of various industries in
eighteen countries.[12] He reasons that the shifts in
industrial structure are hardly surprising "if total
and per-capita product grows . . . the impact on different industries is not likely to be the same."[13]
In short, rapid economic growth in Korea has been
accompanied by an increase in the share of secondary
industry.

Target Growth Rate of GNP

As reviewed in the previous section, Korea has
achieved consistent economic growth since 1954 and
rapid growth in recent years. In the following projection, it is expected that the high growth rate of
GNP will continue in the future. Real GNP is assumed to grow at 8 percent per annum, and the growth
rate remains constant over time throughout the projection period (1967-76). As is true with other

TABLE 2.7

Percentage Shares in Gross National Product
of Industrial Groups

Year	Primary Industry[a]	Secondary Industry[b]	Tertiary Industry[c]
1954	42.0	13.4	44.6
1955	40.5	14.8	44.7
1956	37.4	16.2	46.4
1957	37.9	17.3	44.8
1958	38.5	17.6	43.9
1959	36.4	18.7	44.9
1960	35.2	19.8	45.0
1961	37.4	19.8	42.8
1962	33.4	22.4	44.2
1963	32.5	23.8	43.7
1964	35.1	23.1	41.8
1965	32.3	25.6	42.1
1966	32.3	25.8	40.9
1967	31.8	31.3	40.0
1968	28.9	33.9	37.2

[a] Includes agriculture, forestry, and fishery.

[b] Includes mining, quarrying, manufacturing, construction, electricity, water, gas, transportation,
and communication.

[c] Includes banking, finance, real estate, wholesale
and retail trade, and other services.

Source: The Economic White Paper, Economic Planning
         Board, 1967; Economic Statistics Yearbook
         (The Bank of Korea, 1967); Monthly Economic
         Statistics (The Bank of Korea, November,
         1969).

parameters, the target rate of GNP is chosen through an "iteration process," meaning that the estimates of all relevant variables are calculated simultaneously with different values of parameters, and a reasonable value of each parameter is then selected for the projection.

It is interesting to compare this target rate of growth of GNP with other studies. Our target rate of 8 percent is higher than the target rate of 5 percent set by the United Nations for the "development decade" of the 1960's,[14] but it is lower than the revised target rate of 10 percent set by the Korean Government. (The original target rate in the second plan was 7 percent but was revised upward in 1967.)[15] On the other hand, our target rate is close to the 7.1 percent rate assumed by Fei and Paauw, who break this rate down into 4.3 percent for per-capita income and 2.8 percent for population growth.[16] Rosenstein-Rodan and Chenery and Strout are more pessimistic. Rosenstein-Rodan sets the target growth rate at 3.5 percent for his projection period (1966-71).[17] Chenery and Strout give two alternative target rates of GNP--6 percent as the high value and 4.3 percent as the low value during their projection period (1962-75).[18]

The discrepancy between our target rate and those of Rosenstein-Rodan and Chenery and Strout mainly reflects the fact that theirs covers the period before 1962. They probably did not anticipate the rapid growth of 1962-68. On the other hand, the 10 percent target rate of the Korean Government may be too ambitious under present conditions.

Recent economic performances in Korea show that a new stage of development has been reached. Yet, this achievement does not guarantee the reaching of future targets, including that of self-sustained growth. There still remain many bottlenecks and problems.

One of the main problems in future economic growth in Korea is agricultural production, which is heavily affected by limited arable land.[19] Fortunately

there have been large crops associated with favorable
weather during 1962-68 (except for the crop failure
in 1962). Even moderate degrees of crop failure in
the future will affect the GNP growth rate substantially because the agricultural sector accounts for
about one third of total output and for the liveli-
hood of 55 percent of the population.

Although population growth has slowed down
slightly, it is still a major problem. Family planning is only in the experimental stage despite its
general acceptance by the urban population. Korea
is already overpopulated; the population has swollen
to more than 29 million--crowded into an area slightly smaller than Virginia, whose population is only
4.5 million.[20] Population density is defined as the
number of persons living on a square kilometer (the
world average is 25; the Korean figure is 295). The
population density of Korea in 1966 was almost twelve
times the world average.[21] Unless the population
growth rate declines, there will be detrimental effects on economic development, related both to a high
unemployment rate and low savings and investment
rates.

Inflation is another great threat to the Korean
economy. Inflation tends to "promote the wrong kinds
of investment which are socially undesirable, direct-
ing real resources and productive energies to activities promising high speculative profits in the short
run."[22] Inflation also penalizes savers. Inflation,
as a negative rate of return on savings, constitutes
a punishment levied on suppliers of funds through
organized financial institutions. Consequently, a
strong inflation may often have more harming effects
on growth than benefits.[23]

Finally, as to the bottlenecks, the future supply of raw materials and electric power will certainly have great influence on future growth. Korea is
poorly endowed in natural resources. More than 60
percent of total raw-material needs must be imported.[24] Moreover, the rapid growth rate of the economy as a whole and particularly of manufacturing has
brought about a shortage of electric power. In 1967,

as in some previous years, rapidly rising power consumption and the closing down of some hydroplants
because of protracted drought caused a power gap. As
a result, power consumption of some industries had
to be curtailed.[25]

CAPITAL FORMATION AND ECONOMIC DEVELOPMENT

There are many factors affecting economic development over the longer term. The important factors are capital formation, human skills, education
and training, entrepreneurial innovation, productive
technology, a substantial change in the composition
of output, and the development of new institutions.[26]
But capital formation and investment are still considered the central factors in developing countries.
Moreover, capital-output relationships are much
easier to handle than most other factors, both in
terms of the formal structure of growth models and
for purposes of statistical testing.

The importance of capital formation in developing countries is often stressed by development economists who refer to "vicious circles."[27] The meaning
of vicious circles is expressed in different ways,
but the main concept can be summarized: "A country
is poor because it has little capital, and it cannot
raise capital because it is poor."[28] It is generally
agreed that capital formation takes the top priority
in the strategy of economic development and that "the
process of economic growth and capital accumulation
are closely interconnected whether there is abundant
labor or not."[29] Investment increases output, and
output in turn increases capital formation. The stimulus from added capital formation works like "pump
priming" or a "stimulant" and can generate a break of
vicious circles.

In Korea, investment has played a basic role in
rapid economic growth. As can be seen from Table 2.8,
gross investment increased from 57.87 billion won in
1954 to 344.12 billion in 1968, almost a sixfold increase. Over-all investment was 15.7 percent of
total GNP during the 1954-68 period and helped bring

TABLE 2.8

Output, Investment, and Incremental
Capital-Output Ratio
(in 1965 prices)

Year	GNP	Total Invest- ment	Fixed Invest- ment	ICOR[a] Fixed Capital	ICOR[a] Gross Capital
1954	447.36	57.87	41.66	1.64	2.28
1955	474.54	61.34	48.98	1.80	2.26
1956	480.47	57.29	52.77	8.87	9.63
1957	522.73	87.91	61.31	1.45	2.07
1958	551.69	77.72	57.79	2.00	2.68
1959	575.84	57.83	59.29	2.46	2.39
1960	589.07	62.48	61.71	4.66	4.72
1961	613.61	72.95	65.26	2.66	2.97
1962	634.97	77.99	84.05	3.93	3.65
1963	693.03	137.27	105.95	1.82	2.36
1964	750.31	114.41	93.33	1.63	2.00
1965	805.85	114.48	117.64	2.12	2.13
1966	913.82	207.38	190.63	2.01	2.19
1967	995.16	241.42	232.69	2.30	2.20
1968	1,127.32	344.12	326.53	1.90	2.06

Averages

1954-56	467.46	58.83	47.80	1.72	2.27
1957-61	570.59	71.78	61.07	2.14	2.52
1962-66	759.59	131.07	118.32	1.90	2.17
1954-66	619.48	91.59	80.03	2.18	2.17

[a]Incremental capital-output ratio (ICOR) is the ratio between investment and the change in GNP with a one-year lag. In the calculation of averages, years 1956, 1960, and 1962 are omitted. Unusual conditions, political unrest in 1956 and crop failures in 1956 and 1962, influenced these years. ICOR figures are the three-year moving average.

Source: Calculations from data in The Monthly Statistical Review (The Bank of Korea, July, 1967).

43

about the average GNP growth rate of 6.8 percent per
year. The investment-GNP ratio increased from 12.7
percent in 1957-61 to 19.9 percent in 1962-68, and
the GNP growth rate also jumped in the respective
periods.

As mentioned before, the incremental capital-
output ratio (ICOR) is employed to explain the relationship between investment and output. In our
study, investment figures are gross of depreciations,
because depreciation methods are not generally prac-
ticed and depreciation data are not available. In
Korea, the over-all average ICOR of total investment
including inventories was 2.4 in 1954-58, and the
average of fixed investment was 2.23 in the same period. But these ratios vary in different subperiods.
The average ratio of total investment went up to 2.53
in 1957-61 from 2.27 in 1954-56 and then tended to
decline to 2.17 in 1962-66 and to 2.13 in 1967-68.
The ratio of fixed investment also follows a similar
pattern.

Incremental Capital-Output Ratio

ICOR, using gross investment, is assumed to be
2.0 and to remain constant during the projection
period (1967-76). With an assumed target rate of
GNP at 8 percent and an ICOR of 2.0, the required investment rate is 16 percent of target GNP.

Our estimate of ICOR can be compared with other
estimates. Fei and Paauw's estimate is 3.2, and
Chenery and Strout's is 3.27.[30] One reason why both
estimates are higher than ours lies in the fact that
our estimate excludes the unusually high ratios of
two abnormal years (as explained in Table 2.8). Investment has usually kept up the same rate of increase, while real GNP increased only 1.2 percent in
1956 and 3.5 percent in 1962. Consequently, the ICOR
is 9.63 in 1956 and 3.65 in 1962. Another reason why
Fei and Paauw's estimate differs from ours is that
the former is a combination of (1) the imperfection
of underlying statistical data, (2) the announced
targets of the government, and (3) their own judgment as to the realism of (1) and (2). They use

cross-section analysis of countries as a basis for
the revision of their estimate.[31]

. The selection of the appropriate ICOR for the
future should not simply be based on past averages.
Since the latter part of the 1950's, the ICOR in
Korea has shown a slightly declining tendency.
Leibenstein and Patel have suggested, on the basis
of empirical findings in both developed and underdeveloped countries, that there is an inverse relationship between the ICOR and economic growth.[32]
They suggest that this inverse relationship might be
due to productivity changes and other noncapital inputs, which increasingly contribute to economic
growth. Clark also indicated that the ICOR usually
declines as tertiary industry, which uses less capital, becomes more important in the course of development.[33]

In the case of Korea, the slight downward move-
ment of ICOR remains empirically unexplained. The
future is difficult to project. But it is unreasonable to expect the ICOR to continue to decline below
2.0.

First, in the process of growth, the rate of
return on investment usually diminishes as investment
increases; hence, more investment is required to
achieve the same target growth rate. Second, heavy
investments such as steel complexes, machine factories,
and much social overhead capital are scheduled for
the second- and third-plan periods. Third, the ICOR
in this study is the gross-investment ration, including capital consumption. In the future, old capital
equipment must be properly maintained and eventually
replaced. So far, the assumed ICOR is based on the
constant inventory-output ratio, because inventories
have fluctuated rather randomly.

Investment requirements estimated by the incremental capital-output ratio are a "stimulant" to develop potential economic resources, especially idle
labor, which otherwise stays untapped.[34] In Korea
both unemployment and "disguised" unemployment figures are very high. The unemployment rate was 7.1

percent in 1966, but this figure is misleading because unemployment is defined "to include those who
are fully unemployed, i.e., do not work for even a
single hour of paid work."[35] Therefore, the employment figure includes a substantial number of under-
employed workers in agriculture and other sectors.
The growth potential can be increased by utilizing
idle labor together with new investments.

THE SAVING FUNCTION

Domestic savings both in absolute and relative
terms have been very low in Korea and reflect the low
level of both GNP and per-capita income. But domestic savings have started to increase in the past few
years as the Korean economy entered a new stage of
development.

Table 2.9 shows the increase in the average savings rate from 3.8 percent in 1957-61 to 8.0 percent
in 1962-66 and to 13.7 percent in 1967-68. On an annual basis, the rate has fluctuated widely but has
shown an upward trend since 1962. It may be "too
naive to accept at face value the savings rate [in an]
agricultural economy."[36] When the value added of primary industry declined by 6 percent in 1962, the
average-savings rate also decreased to 1.5 percent.
Since then, the average-savings ratio has continued
to increase.

The increase in the savings rate is partly the
result of growth itself and partly the result of government policies. Most noteworthy of these policies
are financial-stabilization programs, interest rate
and tax reforms during the 1960's. (These reforms
are discussed in detail in Chapter 5.) The government sector had deficits from 1954 through 1962. Government efforts to eliminate deficit financing through
reductions in less urgent expenditures and increases
in tax revenues brought the first positive government
savings in 1964. Surpluses have since continued.
Private savings also increased during 1962-68 when
rapid economic growth occurred in an atmosphere of
relative stability. The establishment of rational

TABLE 2.9

Composition of Savings and Savings Rates
(in billions of won)

Year	Domestic Savings[a] Amount	% of GNP	Government Savings[b] Amount	% of GNP	Private Savings[c] Amount	% of GNP	Marginal Savings Rate[d]
1957	10.93	5.5	-6.01	-3.0	16.94	8.5	19.54
1958	10.27	5.0	-6.43	-3.1	16.70	8.1	-7.01
1959	8.66	3.9	-5.94	-2.7	14.60	6.5	-11.66
1960	3.79	1.6	-5.01	-2.0	8.90	3.6	-18.96
1961	11.32	3.8	-5.30	-1.8	16.62	5.6	15.02
1962	5.17	1.5	-4.86	-1.4	10.03	2.9	-11.88
1963	33.67	6.9	-1.32	-0.3	34.99	7.2	20.45
1964	48.88	7.0	3.55	0.5	45.33	6.5	7.04
1965	60.75	7.5	14.02	1.7	46.73	5.8	11.34
1966	121.32	11.7	29.08	2.8	92.24	8.9	26.78
1967	156.79	12.6	51.86	4.2	87.57	7.1	16.80
1968	235.93	14.9	100.61	6.4	108.01	6.9	23.80
Averages							
1957-61	8.99	3.8	-5.74	-2.4	14.75	5.6	--
1962-66	53.96	8.0	8.09	1.2	45.86	6.8	--
1967-68	196.46	13.7	76.23	5.3	97.79	7.0	20.3

Note: All savings figures include statistical discrepancies.

[a]Domestic savings are the sum of government and private savings.

[b]Negative government savings mean the excess of expenditures over tax revenues.

[c]Private savings include both personal and corporate savings.

[d]Marginal savings rate is a change in gross domestic savings as a percentage of a change in GNP from year to year. Negative marginal savings rates before 1963 are attributable to an absolute decline in total savings as domestic output continued to rise.

Sources: Economic Statistics Yearbook (The Bank of Korea, 1967); Monthly Statistical Review (The Bank of Korea, July, 1967); Monthly Economic Statistics (The Bank of Korea, November, 1969).

interest rates in 1965 helped redirect private savings from hoardings and unorganized money markets to financial institutions. As a result, private savings increased from 2.9 percent of GNP in 1962 to 6.9 percent in 1968. The increases in the average-savings rate and the structural change in domestic savings are also reflected in the increase in marginal-savings rates.

Marginal-Savings Rate

The selection of a marginal-savings rate for projection purposes has been most difficult because of the variability of the rate in the past. But, on the basis of quantitative and qualitative judgment, the marginal-savings rate is assumed to be 18 percent in the first five years (1967-71) and 20 percent the following five years (1972-76) of the projection period. It may be quite possible to have a marginal-savings rate much higher than here estimated in the future, but considering the possible unfavorable factors affecting savings, such as inflation, our estimate is lower than the marginal-savings rate of 20.3 percent in 1967-68. On the other hand, the assumption made exceeds the average rate of 1963-66. It is believed to be plausible, given national determination to increase savings by controlling inflation and by improving the banking and tax systems.

Our estimate of the marginal-savings rate is also compatible with other estimates. Rosenstein-Rodan gives two possible values of the marginal-savings rate, 14 percent in 1966-71 and 18 percent in 1971-76.[37] Fei and Paauw have a projected per-capita marginal rate of 18 percent, while Chenery and Strout have a low value of 15 percent and a high value of 20 percent.[38]

EXPANSION OF EXPORTS

There is a close relationship between international trade and economic development, either from the point of view of comparative advantage or from the viewpoint of an industrialization theory in

developing countries. Exports can become "an engine
of growth"; they played a catalyst role in the economic development of England in the nineteenth century
and of Japan and Taiwan in the twentieth century.[39]

The over-all growth rate of exports of goods
and services in Korea was 17.1 percent per year between 1954 and 1968, but the growth rate in subperiods differed sharply, as can be seen in Table
2.10. During 1954-56, the average annual growth rate
of exports was negative. Korea was preoccupied with
reconstruction of the domestic economy and with meeting critical domestic shortages with limited productive facilities. During 1957-61, there was a change.
After reconstruction efforts began to pay off, a
balanced industrial structure emerged. Export expansion was emphasized as a source of foreign exchange
to finance imports, which had previously been financed
mainly by foreign aid. The average growth in 1957-61
became a positive 16 percent.

An accelerated and dramatic increase in exports
has taken place since the First Five-Year Economic
Plan, especially after 1964. Between 1962 and 1966,
the average growth rate of exports was 21.7 percent
and rose to over 30 percent in 1967-68. The major
contributing factors in export expansion have been
export-promotion measures, including a more realistic
exchange rate, and strong world demand, stimulated
in part by the Vietnam war.

As shown in Table 2.11, the commodity composition of Korean exports has shifted from foodstuffs
and raw materials to manufactured goods. Manufactured goods accounted for 6.6 percent of total exports in 1954-56 and 16.3 percent in 1967-61. A
major increase took place since 1962. The share of
manufactured goods has increased from 19.3 percent
in 1962 to 61.3 percent in 1966. This trend has continued during 1967-68.

Before the Korean War, rice alone accounted for
one third of total exports.[40] The increase in the
proportion of raw materials in the early 1950's was
due to "exports of tungsten, which was used for military weapons."[41]

TABLE 2.10

Exports of Goods and Services
(in millions of U.S. dollars)

Year	Merchan-dise Exports	Sales to U.N. Forces[a]	Other Services	Total Exports	Annual Percentage Change During Period
1954	24.2	34.3	9.9	54.5	-10.9
1955	17.6	44.0	9.7	71.3	10.5
1956	25.1	22.5	15.4	63.0	-11.6
1957	19.4	43.4	15.9	78.7	24.9
1958	17.1	57.6	17.7	92.4	17.4
1959	19.7	63.3	29.6	103.6	12.1
1960	32.8	62.6	21.5	116.9	12.8
1961	40.9	79.7	25.0	145.6	14.6
1962	54.8	86.5	21.9	163.2	12.1
1963	86.6	58.3	30.4	175.5	7.5
1964	119.1	63.7	28.2	211.0	20.2
1965	175.1	74.0	40.7	289.8	37.3
1966	250.3	100.9	103.5	454.7	31.6
1967	334.7	171.4	136.8	642.9	41.4
1968	486.2	216.6	177.5	880.3	36.9

Averages

1954-56	22.3	33.6	11.7	66.2	-4.0
1957-61	26.0	61.3	20.1	107.4	16.4
1961-66	87.2	76.7	44.9	258.6	21.7
1954-66	48.7	60.8	27.7	156.9	13.7
1967-69	410.5	194.0	157.7	761.6	39.7

[a]Sales of goods and services to U.N. Forces stationed in Korea.

Sources: Economic Statistics Yearbook (The Bank of Korea), 1959, pp. 147-48; 1961, pp. 186-87; 1967, pp. 314-17; Monthly Economic Statistics (The Bank of Korea), November, 1969).

TABLE 2.11

Composition of Exports
(in percentages of total value)

Year	Food and Live Animals	Raw Materials	Manufactured Goods	Others
1954	6.4	88.3	3.2	2.1
1955	5.2	86.7	6.0	2.1
1956	5.7	88.1	5.7	0.5
1957	14.9	66.1	18.4	0.6
1958	14.9	67.1	15.6	2.4
1969	20.7	63.9	15.3	0.1
1960	29.6	53.7	16.8	-0.1
1961	19.4	48.1	15.2	17.3
1962	40.0	40.7	19.3	--
1963	20.8	33.5	45.4	0.2
1964	22.1	28.7	49.0	0.2
1965	16.0	22.8	60.9	0.3
1966	16.5	22.1	61.3	0.1
1967	14.0	18.3	67.3	0.4
1968	11.7	14.0	74.7	0.4

Sources: Figures for 1954 were obtained from records of the Ministry of Finance; for 1955 and 1956, figures were based on Economic Statistics Yearbook (The Bank of Korea, 1963); the rest were calculated from Economic Statistics Yearbook, 1966 and 1967 and Monthly Economic Statistics (The Bank of Korea, November, 1969).

51

At present, the diversity of commodity exports gives the impression that much of the export increase of recent years represents solid development. The variety of products is large, and products subject to sudden market changes are few--tungsten and a few other less important minerals and agricultural products. The important and rapid-growth export items are textiles, clothing, raw silk, plywood, human hair and wigs, and steel plates.[42]

The change in the commodity composition of exports is reflected in the terms of trade. The terms of trade in Table 2.12 show a largely unfavorable trend from 1956 to 1961. Since 1962, the trend is reversed, and the change is mainly attributable to structural changes in commodity exports. During 1956-61, a majority of Korean exports consisted of primary goods, which have had a long-term decline in prices.[43] On the other hand, Korean imports before 1961 consisted of a great deal of "capital goods and intermediate raw materials, having a high degree of manufacturing content and higher prices."[44] The improvement in the terms of trade since 1962 is related to the increasing share of manufactured goods in Korean exports and price increases in primary exports.

The value of exports is the combined result of quantity and price changes. For instance, the total value of merchandise exports increased from $86.8 million in 1963 to $250.3 million in 1966, an increase of 186.7 percent over the period. This increase can be explained by a price increase of 16.9 percent and a quantity increase of 146.6 percent. Or, putting it differently, the actual value of merchandise exports might have been smaller had there been no improvement in export prices.

The most important purchasers of Korean goods are the United States and Japan, which accounted for 51.7 percent and 21.9 percent of total exports respectively in 1968. Further diversification, by tapping the European markets as well as markets in the developing world, is of obvious importance.

The recent growth in Korean merchandise and invisible exports is also directly related to the

TABLE 2.12

Foreign Trade and Terms of Trade Index[a]

Year	Export Unit Value Index	Import Unit Value Index	Terms of Trade	Export Quantum Index
	1960 = 100			
1956	156.2	70.5	221.6	27.0
1957	114.5	100.4	114.0	65.1
1958	80.7	85.5	94.4	66.8
1959	85.5	91.6	93.3	71.9
1960	100.0	100.0	100.0	100.0
1961	74.0	85.4	86.7	140.3
1962	100.5	109.6	91.7	147.5
1963	113.9	117.3	97.1	197.5
	1963 = 100			
1963	100.0	100.0	100.0	100.0
1964	102.2	101.2	101.1	134.2
1965	106.1	103.0	103.3	190.1
1966	116.9	103.0	114.7	246.6
	1965 = 100			
1965	100.0	100.0	100.0	100.0
1966	109.1	97.8	111.6	131.0
1967	114.1	98.7	115.6	160.2
1968	117.6	98.3	119.5	221.2

[a]Terms of trade is defined as the ratio of the export unit value over the import unit value index. The terms of trade in which 1960 = 100 were estimated by the Korean Productivity Center, Seoul; the remainder were estimated by The Bank of Korea.

Sources: The Korean Trade Structure and Policies (Seoul: Ministry of Finance, 1967), p. 45; Economic Statistics Yearbook (The Bank of Korea, 1967); Monthly Economic Statistics (The Bank of Korea, November, 1969).

Vietnam war. Commodity exports to Vietnam amounted
to $13.8 million, 6 percent of total exports in 1966.
The percentage is much higher if total current-
account earnings are considered, including transfer
payments ($60.4 million) from Korean military person-
nel and construction and other civilian workers engaged in Vietnam and paid in U.S. dollars.[45] Another
important item in the current account is sales to
U.N. forces stationed in Korea. This item also increased as a result of escalation in the Vietnam con-
flict in 1965. During 1962-64, annual average sales
to U.N. forces amounted to $70 million; and a decline
of such sales was anticipated because of the United
States' "Buy American" policy. However, sales to
U.N. forces increased to $100.9 million in 1966 and
to $177.6 million in 1968.

Export Growth Rate

Exports of goods and services are assumed to
grow at 15 percent per annum, which is much smaller
than the 1962-66 average growth rate of 21.7 percent
and the 1967-68 average of 38 percent. The growth
rate of exports including price increases in the future may be higher than our estimate, which is in
real terms. In the period, export prices increased
by an average of 4 percent per year. On the other
hand, the assumption exceeds substantially the actual growth rate of most developing countries in the
postwar period. (One exception is Israel--perhaps
not classifiable as an underdeveloped country--which
had an annual average rate of export growth of 17
percent in 1950-64.)[46] The Korean Government, however, makes a more optimistic assumption than we do.
The revised target for exports of the Economic Planning Board is $1,074 million in 1971. This means
that exports must grow at approximately 30 percent
per year since 1962.[47]

The basis of their optimism is not reasonable
when likely future changes in international demand
and domestic-supply conditions are taken into account. As mentioned before, Korean exports are concentrated on the United States and Japanese markets.
Korean exports might be severely affected by a small

decrease in purchases by these countries, which might
occur as the consequence of protectionist tendencies
or recessions. (Korean exports accounted for 0.7
percent of U.S. imports and 1.0 percent of Japanese
imports in 1968.)[48] Furthermore, the beneficial effect on imports and invisible earnings of the Vietnam
War must be considered temporary.

On the domestic scene, the anticipated rapid
growth of the economy may lead to a sharp increase in
the demand for manufactured products for domestic
consumption unless domestic consumption is restrained
very severely. At any rate, manufacturing industries
will face serious problems in attempting to expand
their exports by the amounts proposed by the government. Problems common to firms in the export field
are insufficient finance for the required buildup of
larger inventories needed to react promptly to market
opportunities and lack of large, export-trading firms
with worldwide knowledge of trade channels.[49]

Much of the export success in recent years has
been achieved through government promotion. Since
the early 1960's, the government has considered vigorous export growth and the resultant reduction in
the dependence on foreign assistance as chief objectives of economic policy. Credit incentives, tax
incentives, and export subsidies have been used.
Musgrave estimated that export subsidies and other
benefits accounted for 6.1 percent of the total value
of exports in 1964.[50] Thus, another problem is
whether the government is able and willing to continue
bearing the costs of export incentives.

Even when these export incentives are taken into
account, exporting is usually much less profitable
for Korean entrepreneurs than selling in the domestic
market. There is a "dual price system" in which domestic prices are higher than export prices.[51] One
of the purposes of giving export subsidies was to
"enforce" a dual price system to give the exporter
greater flexibility in meeting international competition. But since the 1964 devaluation, domestic prices
and production costs have risen substantially while
the exchange rate has been relatively stable. (See

Chapter 3 for an evaluation of the exchange rate.)
A gradual elimination of export incentives in future
years would further erode export profits and reduce
their competitive strength in the world market unless
the exchange rate were depreciated.

THE IMPORT FUNCTION

As noted, the import function can be viewed as
consisting of two opposing forces--potential-import
demand and import substitution. The two net out to
actual imports, which are expressed as a ratio of
required imports to total output.

Korea's development depends on increasing supplies of imports, especially of capital goods and
raw materials. According to Lewis, the ratio of imports to national income is usually low in a primi-
tive economy before economic development begins, but
it rises rapidly with development. Between 1870 and
1913, the world's real income grew by 2.5 percent to
3 percent while the volume of world imports grew faster, by about 3.25 percent per year.[52] Kindleberger
also notes that in the early stages of development
the ratio of imports to national income rises for the
following reasons, unless restrained by commercial
policy:

> Growth brings new needs which cannot be
> initially supplied locally such as raw
> materials and capital equipment, new appe-
> tites through demonstration effect and
> rising income, and frequently new capacity
> to import through capital-borrowing.[53]

The effect of industrialization on the import
ratio is debatable. Kuznets believes that there is
no clear trend in either direction, but he believes
that the foreign-trade proportion of industrial
countries' national incomes rose from the late nineteenth century to World War I and declined from 1913
to the late 1950's.[54] But how long will it take to
reduce the import ratio of an individual country?
In the case of Great Britain, the import ratio rose

from 18 percent to 29.8 percent in 1900. Then it
took almost sixty years to reduce the ratio to 20.8
percent in 1958.[55]

    In the case of Korea, the import ratio has fluc-
tuated widely over the years. The main reasons for
these fluctuations have been changes in import policies and in available foreign aid. The highest import ratio during the 1954-66 period was 24.46 percent
in 1957, when foreign aid also reached its peak, and
the ratio declined to 15.09 percent in 1961 as foreign aid declined. The import ratio again increased
to 22 percent in 1963, when enlarged imports of investment goods and raw materials were made possible
through the inflow of foreign capital. The ratio
declined sharply to 14.8 percent in 1964, when the
new regime restricted imports except for those contributing to the First Five-Year Economic Plan. The
high ratio of 20.42 percent in 1966 is related to the
increased capacity to import through export earnings
and foreign loans, and by the effect of a "negative
system" which allowed a large number of items to be
imported without quantitative restrictions. Previously, the government employed a "positive system" which
allows imports of only listed items. Under a negative
system, all commodities can be imported except those
listed items.[56]

    The import ratios might have been higher had
there been no import substitution. As can be seen
from Table 2.13, estimated import substitutes increased from $46.5 million in 1960 to $215.3 million
in 1966 and accounted for 2.1 percent of the GNP in
1960 and 5.6 percent in 1966. The estimate of import substitutes is rather arbitrary. Import substitutes are defined as domestic output of those goods
which have been imported previously. This definition
of import substitutes says nothing about the import
demand which may rise faster. At any rate, domestic
output is an additional supply of import-competing
goods without which actual imports might have been
greater. The better estimate for import substitutes
would be value added and would exclude all intermediate inputs such as imports and other materials from
other industries.

TABLE 2.13

Imports and Import Substitution
(in millions of U.S. dollars)

Year	Actual Import[a]		Import Substitution[b]		Potential Import Ratio[c]
	Amount	Ratio	Amount	Ratio	
1954	244.6	15.72	--	--	15.72
1955	377.2	23.00	--	--	23.00
1956	393.9	22.94	--	--	22.94
1957	466.2	24.46	--	--	24.46
1958	403.6	19.83	--	--	19.83
1959	331.1	15.43	--	--	15.43
1960	378.8	17.38	46.5	2.1	19.51
1961	343.0	15.09	52.2	2.3	17.39
1962	452.1	18.84	86.1	3.5	22.34
1963	574.8	22.03	104.6	3.9	25.93
1964	419.6	14.80	134.3	4.6	19.40
1965	486.9	15.21	168.0	5.2	20.41
1966	771.7	20.42	215.3	5.6	26.02

[a]Imports over GNP.

[b]Import substitution is discussed in Chapter 4. Estimates before 1960 are not available.

[c]Imports plus import substitutes divided by GNP; before 1960, without import substitution estimates.

Sources: Economic Statistics Yearbook (The Bank of Korea, 1967); Estimation of Import Substitutes (Seoul: Ministry of Commerce and Industry, 1967).

Import Coefficient

The projection of import requirements is particularly difficult, because of the wide fluctuations of the 1960's, but it has to be attempted. The required import-GNP ratio, with import substitution taken into account, is assumed to be 20 percent in the first five years of the projection (1967-71) and 19 percent in the following five years (1972-76). These estimates--which exceed the average ratio of 18.2 percent in 1962-66--are based on the notion that relative import needs will continue to rise as economic development proceeds. The import-substitution coefficient is projected to increase by 0.5 percent of target GNP each year, the same rate at which it grew in the last five years.

The slight decline in the estimated ratio between 1967-71 and 1972-76 is partly based on such import substitution.[57] Kindleberger argues that when a market grows to a certain size, as measured by total income, opportunity for the development of import substitution is created. This is why import substitution usually takes place after some expansion of exports and imports, which expansion demonstrates the existence of domestic productive capacity and market demand.[58]

There is a time dimension to import substitution, which is related to the need for initial investment in import-substituting industries. Such investment may well require a large import component. Import substitutes from these investments become more important in the long run.

There are additional reasons for assuming a declining import ratio. Engel's law states that the increase in the demand for food and other "inferior" goods will rise less than proportionally to national income. (Food imports still account for about 10 percent of total imports in Korea.) Most social overhead capital--roads, ports, schools--can be provided locally.[59] Finally, the relative growth of services in a rising GNP, which is frequently observed, implies a gradual diversion of expenditures from imports to domestic markets.

Our estimate of import requirements can be compared with other estimates. The revised import target of the Korean Economic Planning Board is $1,372
million in 1972.[60] On our assumption, imports reach
$1,051.6 million in 1971. Our estimate is lower be-
cause it implies an optimistic view on import substitution and assumes more import restrictions on consumer goods. In actual fact, the Korean Government
has recently reversed previous trade-liberalization
measures by increasing the number of commodity imports subject to import quotas.[61] Our estimate of
imports coincides with the mean value of Musgrave's
targets, which range between 22 percent and 15 percent of GNP in 1971.[62] Avramovic, in his projection
of 36 developing countries, treats imports as a residual of exports plus the internal gap. This method
leads to Korean imports of $916.7 million in 1971,
which must assume a more vigorous import-substitution
effect than our estimate. This possibility seems
very unlikely in the case of Korean import substitution.

There is a distinct possibility that imports
will rise beyond projections. As real per-capita income rises, the demand for foreign goods may increase
through the "demonstration effect, modern advertising,
and the rapid changes in communication and transportation."[63] Consequently, the import-GNP ratio will
tend to shift upward. There is also a possibility
that domestic "infant industries" might be unfavor-
ably affected by the inflow of foreign industrial
goods before they can become competitive.

Therefore, protective trade policies are assumed
to continue into the future in Korea from the point
of view that Korea endeavors to industrialize her infant economy through import substitution. Not only
the contemporary advocates of trade protection such
as Singer, Myrdal, Linder, Prebisch, and Hagen, but
also free traders such as Viner and Haberler recog-
nize a valid case for protection in some circumstances.
Some of the valid arguments include the following--
infant industry, economies of scale, external economies, long-run social benefits, and the terms-of-
trade argument.[64] Linder especially advocates the

control of "noninput" imports and even accepts the
balance-of-payments and full-employment arguments for
protection, which are not recognized in the classical
theory.[65]

EXTERNAL-DEBT SERVICE

In this study, debt service is treated as a sep-
arate variable. Debt service represents additional
foreign-exchange needs on top of foreign-capital needs
related to the internal and external gaps discussed
previously.

In recent years, the debt-service problem of
underdeveloped borrower countries has received quite
extensive attention since both external debts and
debt-service obligations have increased.[66] It has
been estimated by the World Bank that public and publicly guaranteed debt of a sample of 37 developing
countries increased from $7 billion at the end of 1955
to $18.2 billion at the end of 1962, i.e., two and a
half times. Amortization and interest payments on
this debt rose from $0.7 billion in 1956 to $2.4 billion in 1963, an almost fourfold increase in seven
years.[67] A 1965 estimate of debt-service requirements
by the United Nations was $3.5 billion.[68]

The main reason for study and debate is to evaluate the debt-servicing capacity of a country in view
of the universal desire to prevent a repetition of
the international debt defaults of the 1930's. According to Avramovic, widespread debt-servicing difficulties arose during the Great Depression of the 1930's
because foreign capital was unproductively invested,
total output decreased, the value of world trade
collapsed in a span of a few years, and new capital
inflow dried up suddenly.[69]

The problem is to determine the debt-service
limit beyond which a country will face difficulties
likely to lead to default. Some analysts use the
ratio of debt service to export proceeds as a tool in
determining the debt-servicing capacity of a country.
But most economists criticize the use of this ratio.[70]

The debt-service ratio is a short-run liquidity indi-
cator. If an individual or a firm is temporarily
short of cash, this does not necessarily imply inabil-
ity to pay back debts in the long run. The appropriate criterion is future earning power of a firm or
an individual. This concept also applies to a country. As Avramovic states:

> The decisive factors are whether debt
> has been incurred for productive pur-
> poses and whether both the loan money
> and the country's own resources have
> been invested in a way which maximizes
> total output and savings and which makes
> the economy more dynamic and resilient.
> The ratio of amortization and interest
> to exports is an indicator of the cash-
> squeeze today and in the immediate fu-
> ture; it has little relevance, if any,
> for long-run analysis.[71]

Therefore, it is not the absolute size of debt-
service requirements that matters but a simultaneous
assessment of all factors determining debt-servicing
capacity in the long run. Linder even accepts the un-
orthodox position that it is acceptable to borrow to
service debt since old loans do not necessarily generate the needed foreign exchange; and he criticizes
the conventional theory that the limit to borrowing
should be the foreign-exchange content of a particular project.[72]

In order to estimate debt-service costs in the
future, the past behavior of relevant variables--
transfer payments, direct investment, and changes in
foreign-exchange reserves--is reviewed below.

Table 2.14 shows that a majority of transfer
payments to Korea consist of official aid. Official aid financed more than 90 percent of the deficits on current account in 1957-62. After 1963,
private transfers began to increase, initially because of remittances of Korean workers employed in
European mines.[73] Following the Vietnam war escalation in 1965, private transfers rose sharply, from

TABLE 2.14

Foreign Capital Inflow and Debt Service
(in millions of U.S. dollars)

Year	Transfer Payments Official[a]	Transfer Payments Private	Direct Investment[b]	Loans Public	Loans Private	Debt Service
1957	358.5	30.8	--	--	--	--
1958	325.8	28.2	--	--	--	--
1959	231.5	18.0	--	12.3	--	--
1960	261.3	20.6	--	5.0	--	--
1961	209.7	26.9	--	3.1	--	--
1962	201.2	37.5	0.6	52.5	1.8	1.08
1963	208.9	57.4	5.4	9.5	54.8	4.41
1964	141.9	56.7	0.8	37.9	61.8	5.98
1965	136.2	74.0	22.6	76.6	83.7	7.36
1966	124.0	103.3	14.5	153.4	104.7	14.39
1967	136.5	101.9	25.0	105.2	150.7	32.30
Total	2,335.5	555.3	68.9	455.5	456.7	65.52

aOfficial transfer payments include various official aids and grants received and sales of agricultural surplus commodities under P.L. 480.

bFigures for loans and direct investment are on an approval basis, not necessarily all disbursed. Foreign loans are medium and long-term capital loans.

Sources: Economic Statistics Yearbook (The Bank of Korea, 1967); Status of Foreign Capital (Seoul: Economic Planning Board, 1967); Monthly Economic Statistics (The Bank of Korea, November, 1969).

$56.7 million in 1964 to $74 million in 1965 and
$103.3 million in 1966. By 1967, there were about
25,000 military and 12,000 civilian personnel stationed in South Vietnam. Total receipts from Vietnam
amounted to $60.4 million in 1966, of which exports
to that country amounted to $13.8 million. The rest
consisted of transfer payments and other invisible
earnings.[74]

Official aid, on the other hand, has declined
since 1957, when U.S. foreign-aid policy shifted emphasis from grants to development-loan programs.[75]
Development loans continued to be emphasized in the
U.S. Foreign Assistance Acts of 1961 and 1967.[76] Direct investment has played a meager role, although
it has risen in recent years.

Foreign loans started to come in after 1959, but
the major increase took place after 1962. Public
loans advanced from $12.3 million in 1959 to $105.2
million in 1967. Private loans rose from an insignif-
icant $1.8 million in 1962 to $150.7 million in 1967.
As a result, debt-service payments increased from
$1.08 million in 1962 to $7.36 million in 1965 and almost doubled to $14.39 million in 1966 as the grace
period on some loans elapsed. Debt service accounted
for 3.1 percent of exports and 0.4 percent of GNP in
1966, which do not seem to be alarming figures.

The size of debt-service payments is determined
by interest rate and amortization schedules negoti-
ated when loans are made. The actual average terms
on Korean external debt are summarized in Table 2.15.
The average interest charge of public debt is 2.6 percent and the average amortization period is about 28.3
years with a grace period of five years. The average interest rate on private debt is about 6 percent,
with an amortization period of 7.6 years and no significant grace period. Public debt with the softest
terms is AID loans, which carry 1 percent interest
and a 40-year repayment period. The hardest terms
are on British Government loans, which call for 5.45
percent interest and 15-year maturity. Some private
loans from Germany and Japan carry a 7 percent interest charge with a maturity of five years.

TABLE 2.15

Average Terms on External Debt[a]
(1955-1966)

	Average Interest	Average Maturity	Grace Period
Public Loans	2.5%	28.3 years	5.4 years
Private Loans	6.0%	7.6 years	--

[a]These averages are the arithmetic averages of representative debt service terms on individual loans.

Source: "Status of Total Foreign Capital Inflow,"
an unpublished statistical compilation of
all loans agreed and approved (Seoul:
Economic Planning Board, 1967).

        Foreign-exchange reserves are indirectly related
to debt service. In our theoretical framework, a
rise in foreign-exchange reserved is viewed as an increase in gross borrowing, after taking into account
exports, imports, and other capital transactions.
Korean exchange reserves have fluctuated from year
to year, but the over-all trend since 1953 has been
upward. Reserves increased from $108.7 million in
1953 to $391 million in 1968 as shown in Table 2.16.
The average ratio of reserves to total imports increased from 31.4 percent in 1953-56 to 41.5 percent
in 1957-61 but declined to about 30 percent in recent
years.

        International reserves have usually decreased
in years of crop failure, as is to be expected. Reserves increased to $207 million in 1961 when there
were two devaluations but also an influx of stabilization funds. The recent increase is attributable
to the expansion of export earnings, net receipts
from private transfers and the inflow of foreign
capital, which indirectly replaced official foreign
borrowing in balancing the balance of payments.[77]

TABLE 2.16

Gold and Foreign-Exchange Reserve

(in thousands of U.S. dollars equivalent)

Year	Total	Gold	Foreign Exchange[a]	Reserve Import Ratio
1953	108,744	1,436	107,312	30.9
1954	107,783	2,328	105,455	44.1
1955	96,078	1,241	94,837	25.5
1956	98,592	1,355	97,237	25.0
1957	115,565	1,457	114,108	24.8
1958	146,482	1,619	144,863	36.3
1959	147,250	1,754	145,496	44.5
1960	157,026	1,830	155,196	41.5
1961	207,045	1,839	205,206	60.4
1962	168,640	1,847	166,793	37.3
1963	131,484	1,851	129,633	22.9
1964	131,672	2,772	128,900	31.4
1965	141,582	3,286	138,296	29.1
1966	239,168	3,381	235,787	31.0
1967	350,579	3,343	347,236	33.5
1968	391,042	3,390	387,652	25.6

[a]Foreign exchange includes U.S. dollars, British pounds, German marks, Canadian dollars, French francs, Italian lire, Swiss francs, Hong Kong dollars, and Japanese yen.

Sources: Economic Statistics Yearbook (Bank of Korea, 1967); Monthly Economic Statistics (Bank of Korea, November, 1969).

Assumptions on Debt Service
and Related Variables

The assumptions on future transfer payments, direct investment, net borrowing, and exchange reserves
are discussed in this section, as are the assumptions
on interest rates and amortization periods on future
external debt.

There are two values for net-transfer payments
in our projection. Net transfers of $154.5 million
annually, 25 percent lower than the present level,
are projected in the first five years (1967-71); and
$103 million, 50 percent less than currently, is pro-
jected for 1972-76. The projection is based on the
notion that foreign aid, except perhaps P.L. 480 on
agricultural surpluses, will gradually decline, but
that private transfer from Korean personnel partici-
pating in the Vietnam war and reconstruction is expected to continue for the foreseeable future. Moreover, there will be private inflows from remittance
of Korean workers in Europe, Korean emigrants, and
private relief organizations.

Another item contributing to future transfers
is Japanese payments. As a result of the Normalization Treaty between Korea and Japan, Japan agreed to
transfer $300 million of Japanese goods and services
on a grant basis. The period of disbursement is
1966-67, at $30 million per year. The Normalization
Agreement with Japan also included, for the same
period, $200 million of soft loans (3.5 percent in-
terest, repayment in 20 years), and at least $300
million in commercial credits.[78]

Foreign direct investment is expected to increase at 10 percent per year. This is a high growth
rate, but the absolute amount resulting from a 10
percent increase on direct investments of $10.7 mil-
lion in 1967 is only $5 million by 1976 and seems
plausible. Direct investment has increased sharply
in recent years as the Korean economy has grown rapidly while the Korean Government has provided favorable legal and tax treatment for foreign investors.
There are now about 100 enterprises in Korea, mostly
in manufacturing, set up with foreign capital or

foreign-equity participation. Plans are final for
nine petrochemical projects with three U.S. firms--
Gulf Oil, Dow Chemical, and Allied Chemical.[79] Ford
and American Motors have participated in joint ven-
tures for automobile plants in Korea. Many other
proposals, including one from the U.S. General Motors,
are under discussion.

Foreign investment is exempt from personal income tax, corporation tax, and property tax--fully
for five years and 50 percent for subsequent years.
Dividends may be fully remitted; up to 20 percent of
the invested capital may be repatriated each year,
beginning two years after the start of operations.[80]

Gross borrowings are assumed to consist of 50
percent public debt (PLD) and 50 percent private
debt (PRD), the ratio that has prevailed in the past.
Similarly, in regard to debt-service terms, the assumptions are based on past-average terms (Table
2.15). Foreign-exchange reserves are expected to
stay at the present 30 percent level of imports. It
is unreasonable to expect that the level will increase because Korea, like many developing countries
"cannot afford the luxury of keeping more reserves,
which could be used for development, in the comparatively idle form of gold and dollar balances."[81]

ESTIMATE OF EXTERNAL-CAPITAL NEEDS

Based on the values of relevant variables and
parameters, a projection of external-capital needs
for Korea for the years 1967-76 is possible. The values are summarized in Table 2.17. By substituting the
values of parameters into the equations given in earlier chapters, we obtain the following relationships:

$$Y_n = Y_o (1 + .08)^n$$

$$I_r = (2) (.08) Y_o (1 + .08)^n$$

$$S_d = S_o + .18 Y_o \left[(1 + .08)^n - 1\right]$$

$$Fk = \left\{(2) (.08) Y_o (1 + .08)^n\right\}$$
$$- \left\{S_o + .18 Y_o \left[(1 + .08)^n - 1\right]\right\}$$

$$M_r = (.20) \, Y_O \, (1 + .08)^n \quad n = 1, \ldots, 5$$

$$= (.18) \, Y_5 \, (1 + .08)^n \quad n = 5, \ldots, 10$$

$$X_n = X_O \, (1 + .15)^n$$

$$FK_n = \left[(.20) \, Y_O \, (1 + .08)^n\right] - \left[X_O \, (1 + .15)^n\right]$$

$$T_n = 154.4 \qquad\qquad n = 1, \ldots, 5$$

$$= 103.3 \qquad\qquad n = 5, \ldots, 10$$

$$DI_n = DI_O \, (1 + .10)^n$$

$$FX_n = .30 \, (M_r)_n$$

$$(i_s)_n = .04 \, (COD_{n-1}) = .04 \, (AOD_{n-1} + AOD_{n-2}$$
$$+ \ldots + APD)$$

$$(COD = \text{cumulative outstanding debt,}$$

$$AOD = \text{annual increase in OD})$$

$$(A_s)_n = \frac{1}{30} \left[PLD_{n-g-1} + \ldots + PLD_{n-g} \right]$$
$$+ \frac{1}{8} \left[PRD_{n-1} + \ldots + PRD_O \right]$$

The results of the calculations based on the above equations are presented in Table 2.18.

Foreign-Capital Needs

As mentioned before, foreign-capital needs (FK) are either the internal gap or the external gap, whichever is larger. The estimates of both gaps, ex ante, are graphically presented in Figure 1. Both decline after 1967, but the external gap declines faster than the internal gap. The reason for the divergence is that, in our model, investment grows faster than imports, and exports increase more rapidly than domestic savings.

The internal gap narrows from $207.7 million in 1967 to $42.1 million in 1976. The external gap

TABLE 2.17

Values of Variables and Parameters in a
Projection of the Korean Economy

Variables in the Base Year (1964–66 average)		Millions of U.S. Dollars
Gross National Product	(Yo)	$3,313.5
Gross Investment	(Ir)	573.2
Gross Domestic Savings	(Sd)	311.5
Exports of Goods and Services	(x)	318.5
Imports of Goods and Services	(Mr)[a]	559.4
Net Transfer	(T)	206.0
Direct Investment, Net	(DI)	8.7
Gross Borrowing	(GD)	93.7
Foreign-Exchange Reserves	(FX)	134.3
Debt Services	(DS)	9.2

Values of Future Parameters (1967–76)

Incremental Capital-Output Ratio	(k)	2
GNP Growth Rate	(r)	8%
Marginal Savings Rate	(s')	18%, 20%
Import-GNP Ratio	(m)	20%, 19%
Export Growth Rate	(x)	15%
Exchange-Reserve Ratio	(f)	30%
Interest Rates	(i_s)	
Public Debt	(PLD)	2.5%
Private Debt	(PRD)	6.0%
Amortization Period	(A)	
Public Debt	(PLD)	30 years
Private Debt	(PRD)	8 years
Grace Period on Public Debt	(g)	5 years

[a]Excludes interest on external debts.

Source: Compiled by the author.

FIGURE 1
Internal and External Gap
(in millions of U.S. dollars)

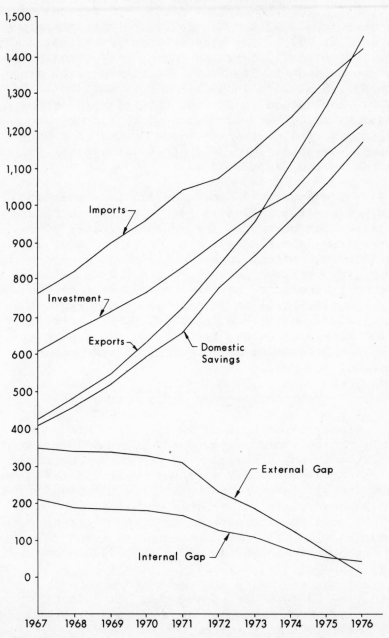

declines from $351.8 million in 1967 to $70.4 million
in 1975, and a surplus of $14.1 million in 1976 is
calculated. Nevertheless, the external gap remains
the larger one until the last year. Therefore, in
estimating foreign-capital needs, the external gap
is used from 1967 through 1975, and the internal gap
is used in 1976. The size of foreign-capital needs
declines steadily over the entire projection period,
as can be seen in Figure 2. Foreign-capital needs
are $351.8 million in 1967 but only $42.1 million in
1976. Dependence on foreign capital will not be
ended by 1976, but the degree of dependence decreases
rapidly. Foreign-capital needs account for only 3
percent of total imports in 1976, as against over two
thirds in the early 1960's.

The change in composition of the projected
foreign-capital inflow is also depicted in Figure 2.
Net-transfer payments, for reasons already given, decline from $154.5 million in 1967-71 to $103 million
in 1972-76. Direct investment increases each year,
from $10.7 million in 1967 to $25.7 million in 1976.
Net borrowings also decline, from $186.6 million in
1967 to $13.9 million in 1974 and become zero there-
after. Net borrowings, however, do not represent
total borrowing needs, because the net figure excludes debt-service requirements and increases in
exchange reserves.

Debt Service and Gross Borrowings

Gross borrowing thus is the key figure. In
1970, for instance, gross borrowings would amount to
$290.1 million, consisting of the following items:
net borrowings ($164.2 million), debt service on past
debt (46.4), interest on cumulative outstanding debt
(28.7), amortization payments on subsequent debts
(37.6), and the increase in exchange reserves (13.3).
Consequently, total external-capital needs (EK) go
up from 392.4 in 1967 to 458.9 in 1970 and decline
very slowly to 321.9 in 1976. (See Table 2.18.) One
noteworthy feature is that debt service on past debt
(existing in 1966) is substantial and cannot be ignored, although Avramovic assumed no such debt existing before his projection.

FIGURE 2
External Capital and Net Foreign Capital
(in millions of U.S. dollars)

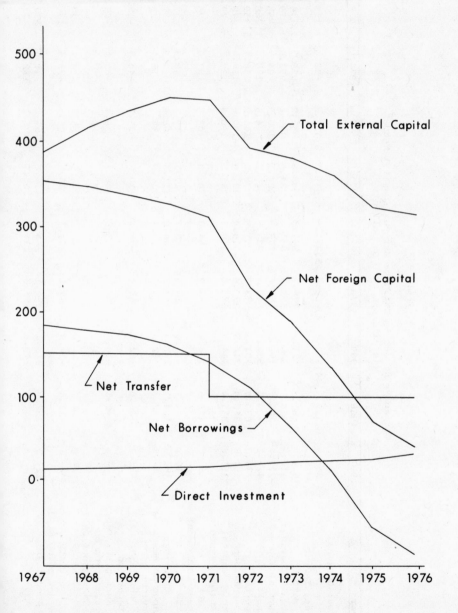

TABLE 2.18

Variables Needed to Estimate External Capital Needs[a]

(in millions of U.S. dollars)

Year	1967	1968	1969	1970	1971	1972	1973	1974	1975	1976
Gross National Product	3,864.9	4,173.9	4,507.8	4,864.4	5,257.9	5,678.5	6,132.8	6,623.4	7,153.3	7,725.6
Gross Investment	618.4	667.8	721.2	778.9	841.3	908.6	981.2	1,059.7	1,144.5	1,236.1
Domestic Savings	410.7	466.3	526.4	591.3	661.4	784.5	875.4	973.5	1,079.5	1,194.0
Internal Gap	-207.7[b]	-201.5	-194.8	-187.6	-179.9	-124.1	-105.8	-86.2	-65.0	-42.1
Exports	421.2	484.4	557.1	640.7	736.8	847.3	974.4	1,120.6	1,288.7	1,482.0
Imports	773.0	834.8	901.6	973.7	1,051.6	1,078.9	1,165.2	1,258.4	1,359.1	1,467.9
External Gap	-351.8	-350.4	-344.5	-333.0	-314.8	-231.6	-190.8	-137.8	-70.4	+14.1
Foreign Capital	351.8	350.4	344.5	333.0	314.8	231.6	190.8	137.8	70.4	42.1
Transfer Payments, Net	154.8	154.8	154.8	154.8	154.8	103.0	103.0	103.0	103.0	103.0
Direct Investment, Net	10.7	11.8	13.0	14.3	15.7	17.3	19.0	20.9	23.0	25.3
Net Borrowings	186.6	184.1	177.0	164.2	144.6	111.3	68.8	13.9	-55.6	-86.2
Change in Reserves	11.9	12.3	12.8	13.2	13.9	14.0	14.7	15.1	15.5	15.9
Services of Past Debt	-28.7	-36.0	-40.6	-46.4	-37.5	-30.2	-35.2	-40.5	-45.3	-50.0
Interest on Subsequent Debt	--	-9.1	-18.8	-28.7	-38.8	-48.2	-56.4	-63.4	-68.7	-71.6
Amortization on Subsequent Debt										
Public[c]	--	--	--	--	--	-4.5	-9.6	-15.1	-20.9	-26.6
Private	--	-11.4	-24.0	-37.6	-52.1	-66.6	-80.3	-93.6	-105.7	-115.7
New Borrowing Needs										
Annual Gross	227.2	252.9	273.2	290.1	286.9	274.8	265.0	241.6	200.5	193.6
AOD	--	241.5	249.2	252.5	234.8	203.7	175.1	132.9	73.9	51.3

Year	1967	1968	1969	1970	1971	1972	1973	1974	1975	1976
Cumulative Outstanding	--	468.7	719.9	970.4	1,205.2	1,408.9	1,584.0	1,716.9	1,790.8	1,842.1
Debt Services as Percent of Exports	6.8	11.7	20.0	17.6	17.4	17.6	18.6	19.0	18.7	17.8
as Percent of GNP	0.7	1.4	1.9	2.3	2.4	2.6	3.0	3.2	3.4	3.4

[a] Computations are based on the framework in Chapter 1 and values of variables and parameters in Table 2.17. The format is the revised version of D. Avramovic's growth and external debt model.

[b] (-) means net outflow in the balance-of-payments account.

[c] No public debt amortization 1967-71 because of a five-year grace period.

Source: D. Avramovic, Economic Growth and External Debt (Baltimore: Johns Hopkins Press, 1964), pp. 156-57.

As can be seen from Figure 3, gross borrowings reach a peak of $290.1 million in 1970 and then decline each year, amounting to $193.6 million in 1976. The annual increase in outstanding debt (AOD) also reaches a peak of $252.5 million in 1970 and declines to $51.3 million in 1976. But cumulative outstanding debt continues to increase and amounts to $1.8 billion in 1976.

Although Korea is not a representative of developing countries, it follows the general pattern of the debt cycle set out by Avramovic. The debt cycle, according to Avramovic, shows rising indebtedness in the first twenty-five years, and outstanding debt becomes zero in the thirty-sixth year. The net-capital inflow in Korea declines, and total outstanding debt increases in 1967-76. But it is unreasonable to expect that cumulative outstanding debt in Korea becomes zero in thirty-six years from 1967.

On the whole, annual-gross borrowings are larger than the internal or external gap, mainly because of increasing amount of debt service over the period. Consequently, external-capital needs are also greater than the internal or external gap. But the rate of increase in gross borrowings and external-capital needs decreases after 1970, as the larger part of total investment is being financed by domestic savings, and export earnings are used to finance not only the larger part of import requirements but also debt-service payments. The changes of these variables over the years are a better tool than a debt-service ratio, which is a static analysis for evaluating the country's debt-servicing capacity.

It may be concluded that, as far as this model goes, the burden of debt service will not reach a danger point and that Korea will be able to pay back external debts in the long run if the assumptions underlying the parameter estimates are reasonable. Although the debt-service ratio reaches a maximum of 20 percent in 1969, and although this figure exceeds the present debt-service limit of 9 percent set by the government,[82] exports are higher than ever and the debt-servicing capacity ratio, even at the maximum, remains in the middle range of the ratio for a sample of underdeveloped countries.[83]

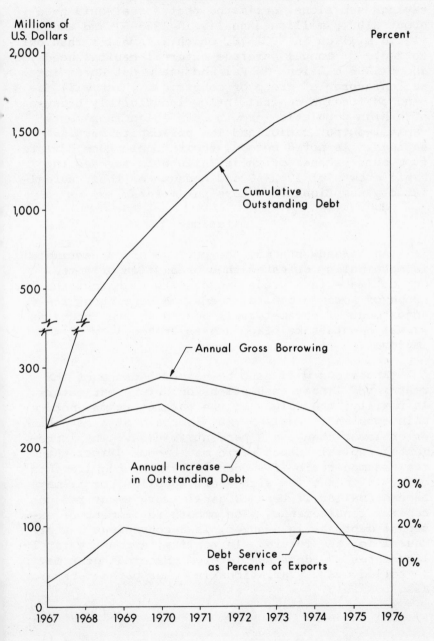

FIGURE 3
External Debt and Debt Service
(in millions of U.S. dollars)

Millions of
U.S. Dollars

Percent

2,000 —

1,500 —

1,000 —

Cumulative
Outstanding Debt

500 —

Annual Gross Borrowing

300 —

200 —

Annual Increase
in Outstanding Debt

30 %

20 %

100 —

Debt Service
as Percent of Exports

10 %

0 —
1967 1968 1969 1970 1971 1972 1973 1974 1975 1976

It is rather difficult to compare our estimate
of external-capital needs with other studies which
do not treat debt service and exchange-reserve needs
separately. Rosenstein-Rodan, using the investment-
savings gap alone, estimated that Korea would need
about $100.8 million annually in 1966-67 and about
$121.8 million in 1971-76, which is smaller than our
estimate of annual, average external-capital needs of
about $396 million.[84] Fei and Paauw put Korea into
an "unfavorable" group of countries, which will depend on foreign-capital inflow indefinitely because
of a high population-growth rate, high incremental
capital-output ratio, and low per-capita marginal
savings. As noted before, their conclusions deviate
from ours because of their failure to foresee the
rapid growth of 1962-68 and because of their unrealistic assumptions on future parameters.

Limitations

As already stated, the purpose of our estimate
is more policy oriented than prediction oriented.
Our estimate is a crude exercise to highlight the
scope of Korea's capital needs. A continuous re-
adjustment of parameters is needed in the future as
actual events take place and as the quality of data
improves.

Revisions will also be needed because of the
restricted linear assumptions on future parameters.
In reality, the values of the parameters may not remain constant. Real GNP may increase at a rate higher or lower than the 8 percent assumed. The incremental capital-output ratio may become larger than
the assumed ratio if sudden investment requirements
occur in industries with short supplies, or it may
become smaller if technological improvement reduces
capital requirements. The smooth retirement of external debt, as is assumed, is a convenient way of
describing the future. In reality, a country rarely
liquidates its debt completely. External debt may
be rolled over. Variations in other parameters are
also possible.

Sensitivity of the Estimates
to Parameter Values

The impact on the amount of foreign-capital needs of the variability of parameters can be discussed in terms of a sensitivity analysis. The sensitiveness of the model to changes in parameters can be shown with our equations. Take the following original equation for internal gap:

$$FK = \left[kr \ (Y_O) \ (1 + r)^n \right]$$
$$- \left[So + s' \left\{ Y_O \ (1 + r)^n - Y_O \ (1 + r)^{n-1} \right\} \right]$$
$$= \left[kr \ (Y_O) \ (1 + r)^n \right]$$
$$- \left[So + s' \ Y_O \left\{ (1 + r)^n - 1 \right\} \right] \tag{9}$$

By partially differentiating the above expression with respect to each parameter--holding everything else constant--and then substituting actual values for parameters, we get the following expressions:

$$\frac{dFK}{dr} = kY_O \ (1 + r)^n + k \ r \ Y_O \ n \ (1 + r)^{n-1}$$
$$- s' \ Y_O \ n \ (1 + r)^{n-1}$$
$$= 2.06 \ Y_O \ (1 + .18)^{n-1} \tag{9a}$$

$$\frac{dFK}{dk} = r \ (Y_O) \ (1 + r)^n$$
$$= .08 \ (Y_O) \ (1 + .08)^n \tag{9b}$$

$$\frac{dFK}{ds'} = Y_O \ (1 + r)^n - 1 = - Y_O \ (1 + .08)^n -1 \tag{9c}$$

These equations show that foreign-capital needs are positively sensitive to the GNP growth rate (9a) and the incremental capital-output ratio (9b), and negatively sensitive to the marginal-savings rate (9c).

The sensitiveness of foreign-capital needs can also be expressed through the external-gap equation:

$$FK = m\,(Y_O)\,(1 + r)^n - X_O\,(1 + x)^n \qquad (12)$$

Again partially differentiating the above equation with respect to each parameter, holding everything constant and then substituting actual values for parameters, we get the following expressions:

$$\frac{dFK}{dr} = m\,Y_O\,n\,(1 + r)^{n-1}$$

$$= .20\,Y_O\,n\,(1 + .08)^{n-1} \qquad (12a)$$

$$\frac{dFK}{dm} = Y_O\,(1 + r)^n = Y_O\,(1 + .08)^n \qquad (12b)$$

$$\frac{dFK}{dx} = X_O\,n\,(1 + x)^{n-1}$$

$$= -Y_O\,n\,(1 + .15)^{n-1} \qquad (12c)$$

It is obvious that debt-service payment is also sensitive to changes in the interest rate and the amortization period, from the following equations:

$$DS_n = (DS_p)_n + i\,(COD)_{n-1}$$

$$+ \frac{1}{t}\left[GD_{n-g-1} + \cdots + GD_{n-g} \right] \qquad (13)$$

$$\frac{dDS}{di} = COD_{n-1} \qquad (13a)$$

$$\frac{dDS}{dt} = \frac{1}{t^2}\,(GD_{n-g-1} + \cdots$$

$$+ GD_{n-g}) \qquad (13b)$$

One note of caution is required with regard to these partial derivatives. They show the impact on foreign-capital needs of an infinitesimal change in each parameter.* To find the change in foreign-capital requirements after a relatively large percentage change in a parameter, interpolation is

---

*The impact on foreign capital of an infinitesimal change in the GNP growth rate, for instance, is equivalent to $dFK = dr \cdot (2.06)\,Y_O\,(1 + .08)^n$

TABLE 2.19

Changes in External Capital Needs Under Various Parameter Values[a]
(in millions of U.S. dollars)

Year	Target Rate of GNP (7%)	Incremental Capital-Output Ratio (2.5%)	Marginal Savings Rate (20-22%)	Assumed Value of Changed Parameters[b]			Amortization Period[c]	
				Import GNP Ratio (21-20%)	Export Growth Rate (13%)	Interest Rate (5%)	Public Debt (25%)	Private Debt (7%)
1967	- 14.3	155	-10	54	14	--	--	--
1968	- 24.3	167	-18	66	24	2.3	--	1.6
1969	- 36.4	181	-24	80	38	4.6	--	3.4
1970	- 51.4	195	-32	97	54	7.2	--	5.4
1971	- 68.7	211	-39	115	74	9.7	--	7.5
1972	-85.9	227	- 7	132	98	12.1	0.9	9.4
1973	-109.2	246	-17	156	127	14.0	1.9	10.4
1974	-136.9	266	-26	181	164	15.8	3.0	13.2
1975	-169.6	285	-37	210	208	17.1	4.2	14.9
1976	-259.9	309	-65	242	260	17.9	5.4	16.4

aAll parameter values in Table 2.17 are retained except that in Column 1 of this table.
bparameters with two numbers connected by (-) denote the first number for the first
five years and the second number for the rest of period.
cThe number of years.

Source: Compiled by the author.

recommended. For instance, lowering the target rate of GNP to 7 percent from 8 percent, ceteris paribus, reduces foreign-capital needs by $75.8 million in 1971. Raising the incremental capital-output ratio to 2.5 raises required foreign capital by $210.3 million in 1971. Increasing the marginal-savings rate to 20 percent decreases foreign-capital requirements by $39 million in 1971. Table 2.19 shows the changes in external-capital needs with different but still defensible parameters.

The same type of interpolation can be illustrated with respect to the external gap and debt service. Raising the import-GNP ratio to 21 percent increases foreign-capital needs by $56.8 million in 1971. Foreign-capital requirements decrease by $39.4 million in 1971 when exports grow at 16 percent per year. Finally, when the average interest on new borrowings is raised to 5 percent, debt service increases by $9.7 million in 1971.

NOTES

1. See Review of Long-Term Economic Projections for Selected Countries in the ECAFE Region (Bangkok: United Nations Economic Commission for Asia and the Far East, 1964), pp. 4-5.

2. The Second Five-Year Economic Development Plan (1967-71) (Seoul: Government of the Republic of Korea, 1966), pp. 33-34.

3. John Pincus, Trade, Aid, and Development (New York: McGraw-Hill, 1967), p. 300.

4. D. Avramovic, Economic Growth and External Debt (Baltimore: Johns Hopkins Press, 1964), pp. 47-53.

5. Ibid., p. 5.

6. Pincus, op. cit., p. 300.

7. Ibid., p. 301.

8. The Korean Trade Structure and Policies
(Seoul: Ministry of Finance, 1967), p. 71.

9. Second Five-Year Economic Plan, op. cit.,
pp. 18-19.

10. See W. Arthur Lewis, The Theory of Economic
Growth (London: George Allen & Unwin, 1955), pp.
420-21; Harvey Leibenstein, Economic Backwardness
and Economic Growth (New York: John Wiley & Sons,
Inc., 1963), p. 7; and Simon Kuznets, Modern Economic
Growth (New Haven: Yale University Press, 1966), pp.
19-20.

11. Colin Clark, Conditions of Economic Growth
(3rd ed.; London: Macmillan, 1951), Chapters 4
and 5.

12. Kuznets, op. cit., pp. 86-93.

13. Ibid., p. 86.

14. Proceedings of the U.N. Conference on Trade
and Development (UNCTAD), V (New York, 1964), pp.
3-10.

15. See Second Five-Year Plan, op. cit., p. 9;
Hankook Ilbo (Korean daily newspaper), March 15, 1968.

16. John C. H. Fei and Douglas S. Paauw,
"Foreign Assistance and Self-Help: A Reappraisal of
Development Finance," The Review of Economics and
Statistics (August, 1965), p. 262.

17. P. N. Rosenstein-Rodan, "International Aid
for Underdeveloped Countries," The Review of Economics and Statistics (May, 1961), p. 120.

18. H. B. Chenery and A. M. Strout, "Foreign
Assistance and Economic Development," The American
Economic Review (September, 1966), p. 713.

19. Leibenstein, op. cit., pp. 38-41.

20. The population of Virginia is from Statistical

Abstract of the United States (Washington, D.C.: U.S. Government Printing Office, 1967), p. 12.

21. *Demographic Yearbook* (United Nations, 1966), pp. 95-106.

22. Arthur I. Bloomfield, *A Report and Recommendations on Monetary Policy and Banking in Korea* (Seoul: Bank of Korea, 1965), pp. 104-9).

23. See Graeme S. Dorrance, "The Effect of Inflation on Economic Development," *IMF Staff Papers* (March, 1963), pp. 2-3; and Tom E. Davis, "Inflation and Growth in Latin America," *Economic Development and Cultural Change* (July, 1966), pp. 506-11.

24. *Industrial Reports* (Seoul: Korean Reconstruction Bank, 1966), p. 44.

25. *Hankook Ilbo, op. cit.*, April 16, 1968.

26. Modern treatments of economic development include Lewis, *op. cit.*, pp. 7-21; W. Rostow, "The Take Off into Self-Sustaining Growth," *Economic Journal* (March, 1965), pp. 25-48; and H. W. Singer, *International Development* (Parts I and II; New York: McGraw-Hill, 1964).

27. For instance, Singer, *op. cit.*, p. 26; also see Ragner Nurske, *Problems of Capital Formation in Underdeveloped Countries* (New York: Oxford University Press, 1961), pp. 4-5.

28. Leibenstein, *op. cit.*, p. 95.

29. A. K. Cairncross, "Capital Formation in Take-Off," in W. W. Rostow (ed.), *The Economics of Take-Off into Sustained Growth* (New York: St. Martin's Press, 1963), pp. 240-60.

30. Fei and Paauw, *op. cit.*, p. 262; Chenery and Strout, *op. cit.*, p. 713.

31. Fei and Paauw, *loc. cit.*

32. Harvey Leibenstein, "The Incremental-Capital-Output Ratio," Review of Economics and Statistics (February, 1966), pp. 20-25; and Surendra J. Patel, "A Note on the Incremental Capital-Output Ratio and Economic Growth in Developing Countries," Kyklos, Vol. XXI, pp. 147-50.

33. Clark, op. cit., pp. 500-4.

34. Norman S. Buchanan and Howard S. Ellis, Approaches to Economic Development (New York: The Twentieth Century Fund, 1955), pp. 21-22.

35. Second Five-Year Plan, op. cit., p. 68.

36. Economic Whitepaper (Seoul: Economic Planning Board, 1967), p. 155.

37. Rosenstein-Rodan, op. cit., p. 133.

38. Fei and Paauw, op. cit., p. 262; Chenery and Strout, op. cit., p. 713.

39. Ragner Nurske, Equilibrium and Growth in the World Economy (Cambridge: Harvard University Press, 1961), pp. 245-47; Joseph T. C. Chao, "Taiwan's Economic Growth: A Case Study of Trade Expansion Policy," unpublished dissertation, New York University Graduate School of Business Administration, 1967), pp. 70-71.

40. H. C. Wu, Prewar and Postwar Trade Pattern of Korea (Washington, D.C.: International Monetary Fund, 1949), p. 2.

41. Balance of Payments of Korea (Seoul: Bank of Korea, 1967), pp. 82-83.

42. These items are obtained from "Exports by Commodity Group and Commodity," Economic Statistics Yearbook (Seoul: Bank of Korea, 1967), pp. 266-75.

43. See R. Prebisch, "Towards a New Trade Policy for Development," Proceedings of UNCTAD, op. cit.,

Vol. II (1964), pp. 15-30; R. Prebisch, "Commercial Policy in the Underdeveloped Countries," The American Economic Review (May, 1959), pp. 251-73; and Singer, op. cit., pp. 161-72.

44. Korean Trade Structure and Policies, op. cit., pp. 44-45.

45. Significant Economic Indicators (Seoul: Economic Planning Board, 1967), p. 152.

46. Pincus, op. cit., p. 74.

47. Overall Resources Budget: 1968 (Seoul: Economic Planning Board, 1968), p. 25.

48. Monthly Bulletin of Statistics, United Nations (June, 1968), pp. 102-6.

49. Staffan Burenstam Linder, Trade and Trade Policy for Development (New York: Frederick A. Praeger, 1967), p. 38.

50. Peggy Musgrave, Trade Targets and Policies in Korea's Economic Development (Seoul: Economic Planning Board, 1965), p. 53.

51. Thomas H. Tudor, "Export Promotion Measures," in Nathan Product Series (Seoul: Economic Planning Board, 1965), pp. 12-13. Nathan Product Series is a collection of papers submitted by economic consultants of the Robert R. Nathan Economic Advisory Group.

52. Lewis, op. cit., pp. 342-45.

53. Charles P. Kindleberger, Foreign Trade and the National Economy (New Haven: Yale University Press, 1962), p. 184.

54. See Kuznets, op. cit., pp. 312-19.

55. Prebisch, "Towards a New Trade Policy," op. cit., p. 5; Industrialization and Foreign Trade (Geneva: League of Nations, 1945) pp. 157-67; Korean Trade Structure, op. cit., p. 22.

56. Korean Trade Structure, op. cit., pp. 56-60.

57. Kindleberger, op. cit., p. 186; Hollis B. Chenery, "Patterns of Industrial Growth," The American Economic Review (September, 1960), pp. 342-45.

58. Arthur Lewis, Development Planning (New York: Harper & Row, 1966), pp. 38-40; Albert D. Hirschman, The Strategy of Economic Development (New Haven: Yale University Press, 1958), pp. 120-22.

59. Kindleberger, op. cit., p. 185.

60. Overall Resources Budget, op. cit., p. 25.

61. Allocation of Foreign Exchanges for Imports (Seoul: Ministry of Commerce and Industry, 1968), pp. 1-67; Hankook Ilbo, op. cit., May 29, 1968 and March 9, 1970.

62. Musgrave, op. cit., pp. 12-13.

63. Nurske, Problems of Capital Formation, op. cit., pp. 58-59.

64. The arguments for and against protection are clearly stated by Linder and Pincus; see Linder, op. cit., pp. 121-38.

65. Ibid.

66. G. M. Alter, "The Servicing of Foreign Capital Inflows by Underdeveloped Countries," in H. S. Ellis and H. C. Wallich, eds., Economic Development for Latin America (New York: Macmillan & Co., 1963), pp. 139-55; D. Avramovic, Debt Servicing Capacity and Postwar Growth in International Indebtedness (Baltimore: Johns Hopkins Press, 1958); D. Avramovic and R. Gulhati, Debt Servicing Problems of Low-Income Countries (Baltimore: Johns Hopkins Press, 1960); and "Economic Growth and External Debt: A Statistical Presentation," submitted by the International Bank for Reconstruction and Development (IBRD or the World Bank), at the 1964 UNCTAD meeting in Geneva, Proceedings of UNCTAD, op. cit., Vol. IV.

67. Avramovic, Economic Growth and External Debt, op. cit., p. 4.

68. External Financing of Economic Development (New York: United Nations, 1968), p. 51.

69. Avramovic, Economic Growth and External Debt, op. cit., p. 6.

70. Ibid., pp. 38-39; for other examples, also see Alter, op. cit., pp. 145-46; Avramovic, Debt Servicing Problems, op. cit., Introduction; and David Finch, "Investment Service of Underdeveloped Countries," IMF Staff Papers (1951), pp. 60-85.

71. Avramovic, Economic Growth and External Debt, op. cit., p. 43.

72. Linder, op. cit., pp. 117-18 and footnote 47, p. 167.

73. Balance of Payments, op. cit., pp. 92-93.

74. Significant Economic Indicators, op. cit., p. 152.

75. Monthly Statistical Review (Seoul: Bank of Korea, October, 1965), pp. 24-25.

76. New York Times, February 10, 1967.

77. Economic Whitepaper, op. cit., p. 66.

78. Review of Korean Economy, 1967 (Seoul: Bank of Korea, 1968), p. 158.

79. Hankook Ilbo, op. cit., March 27, 1968.

80. Foreign Capital Inducement Law (Seoul: Economic Planning Board, 1966), pp. 8-9.

81. Maxwell Stamp, "The Stamp Plan," in Robert G. Hawkins, ed., Compendium of Plans for International Monetary Reform, The Bulletin, No. 37-38 (New York University Graduate School of Business Administration, December, 1965), pp. 62-63.

82. <u>Monthly Statistical Review</u>, <u>op. cit.</u>
(October, 1965), pp. 24-26; and <u>Significant Economic
Indicators</u>, <u>op. cit.</u>, p. 22.

83. Avramovic, <u>Economic Growth and External
Debt</u>, <u>op. cit.</u>, pp. 44-45.

84. Rosenstein-Rodan, <u>op. cit.</u>, p. 133.

CHAPTER **3** FACTORS AFFECTING
EXPORTS

INTRODUCTION

As shown in Chapter 2, Korean exports have
grown at an unbelievably high rate, and the assumption about the future growth rate in the projections
of the model is also high. This chapter will examine
some of the forces operating on exports in the past,
assess the prospects for the future, and evaluate
government policies relating to them.

Developing countries are faced with the two
horns of dilemma between the classical adherents of
free trade and those with interventionist arguments.
In the case of Korea, it has opted for the interventionist route toward industrialization as this chapter will show.

Broadly speaking, the classical theory, which
was popular in the nineteenth century, emphasized the
supply side as the major determinant of exports.
Specifically, the classical doctrine of free trade
states that a country should export those commodities
in which it has a comparative advantage. By spe-
cializing in labor-intensive commodities, exports can
become an "engine" of growth. In the nineteenth century, the supply was the source of growth because the
foreign demand for primary products in the region of
recent settlement (RRS)--Canada, Argentina, Australia,
New Zealand, South Africa, and the United States--was
sufficient.[1]

In the twentieth century, the international-
demand conditions confronting primary goods of LDC's
have changed. Modern economists with a special

interest in LDC's, such as Singer, Nurske, Prebisch,
Linder, and Pincus, have expressed a pessimistic
view on the usefulness of the LDC's exports as a
"lead" sector in economic growth. According to recent calculations by Pincus, the share of industrial
countries in total world exports increased from 66
percent in 1950 to 78 percent in 1965, while that of
LDC's decreased correspondingly.[2] In other words,
the industrial countries have not been transmitting
the growth implicit in rising trade among themselves
to developing countries through a proportional increase in their demand for primary products--but the
world demand for manufactures is bouyant.

Nurske gives the following reasons for the lag-
ging international demand for primary products:

1. The increasing importance of heavy
   industries in industrial countries.
   These require less raw materials per
   unit of output than light industry.

2. The rising share of services in the
   total output of advanced industrial
   countries.

3. The low-income elasticity of demand
   for many primary commodities.

4. Protective tariffs in industrial
   countries.

5. Synthetic and other manmade substitutes for natural materials.[3]

Prebisch adds to these arguments the one that
the terms of trade for primary commodities have tended to deteriorate over the long run.[4] Because the
supply of primary products is inelastic, prices of
these products decline severely during recessions,
while prices of manufactures are relatively stable
as their supply is more elastic. Where the demand
for primary products is also price or income inelastic, an increase in the production of primary goods
through additional labor and capital in traditional

export sectors will lead to further deterioration in
the terms of trade.[5] Singer argues that "technical
progress in manufacturing industries shows up in a
rise in incomes, while technical progress in the production of food and raw materials in underdeveloped
countries showed in a fall in prices."[6] This can be
explained by the constant, downward pressure on wages
from abundant labor in LDC's and by monopolistic
union power in industrial countries.

The conclusion drawn from these circumstances by
many developing countries, including Korea, is that
exports of manufactures rather than that of primary
products to developed countries should be encouraged.
The United Conference on Trade and Development
(UNCTAD), headed by Prebisch, has frequently recommended tariff preferences for LDC's manufactured
products.[7] Concurrently, a part of the economically
active population now in agriculture would have to
be shifted to industry in the LDC's.

It may be a logical economic strategy for dense-
ly settled areas like Korea, where labor is abundant,
to promote exports of labor-intensive manufactures.
Thus, advantages might be taken of the expansion of
world demand for manufactures without reducing imports
of manufactures. According to the Hilgerdt findings,
industrialization in LDC's did not encroach upon total imports of manufactures from the old countries.[8]
This would also imply, however, displacement of "high-
cost supplies in the older industrial countries who
would shift to more productive and more rewarding
lines of activity such as skilled services, engineer-
ing, and chemistry."[9] In reality, however, the introduction of manufactures (textiles, for instance) from
poor into rich countries usually brings about protests
by the industries affected in the wealthy countries
and hence protective measures. This consideration is
therefore an important factor affecting economic
strategy in the LDC's.

LABOR PRODUCTIVITY AND WAGE COMPARISONS

Actually, to be more complete in the analysis of
factors affecting Korean exports, both the supply and

demand function should be dealt with. The high
growth in Korean exports, which rose much faster than
world trade, indicates a high degree of international
competitiveness and rapidly expanding supply. One
indication of competitiveness is productivity and
wage rates--or labor cost per unit.

As mentioned before, labor-cost comparisons
rather than money-wage comparisons alone are the meaningful indicators of competitiveness in the world
market. Output per manhour measures the combined
productivity of labor and capital as well as manageri-
al factors. Wages are only one aspect of total productivity.

Comparative studies by MacDougal and Balassa
suggest that the United States has tended to export
those commodities in which its labor productivity and
wages exceeded those of England by the largest mar-
gins.10 For products where these indexes were relatively less above those of England, the bulk of the
export markets was held by Great Britain. Balassa
concluded that the evidence is less clear when the
comparison is made in terms of wage differentials
than when it is made in terms of labor-productivity
differentials.

Theoretically, productivity improvement is reflected in lower prices and higher quality of goods
and services. It is well known, however, that Korean
exports are facing difficulties in international competition. Production costs are high for reasons other
than wages. The scarcity of capital is reflected in
interest rates as high as 30 percent--a figure of
course also influenced by inflation--and costs are
also high owing to inefficient management.

Table 3.1 shows the number of manhours required
to produce a unit of a few representative manufactures
in Korea and Japan. Korea is superior in none and
comes close in only a few cases. Even in textiles--
a well-established industry in Korea--manufacturing
productivity is lower than in Japan. Similar obser-
vations apply to the paper and cement industries.
Relative labor productivity in Korea is lowest in
heavy-investment goods, such as metal and machinery.

TABLE 3.1

Labor Productivity in Korea and Japan

Industry	Manufactures	Unit[a]	Required Manhours				A/B
			Korea	(A)	Japan	(B)	
Textiles	Cotton	yd	3.64	(1965)	2.16	(1963)	1.7
Paper	Paper	mt	52.19	(1965)	16.47	(1963)	3.2
Rubber	Tires	mt	188.90	(1964)	92.57	(1963)	2.0
Chemicals	Caustic Soda	mt	48.59	(1965)	14.46	(1963)	3.4
Cement & Glass	Cement	mt	1.66	(1964)	1.11	(1963)	1.5
Basic Metals	Steel Plate	mt	22.37	(1965)	2.64	(1963)	8.5
Machinery	Bearings	mt	938.48	(1964)	124.69	(1963)	7.5

[a]yd = yard; mt = metric ton.

Source: Estimate of Labor Productivity in Korean Manufacturing (Seoul: Korean Productivity Center, 1967), p. 19.

94

Specialization in light industry in the LDC's and in
heavy industry in advanced countries is clearly indicated.

Further, empirical support for such specialization is given by the data in Table 3.2. Labor productivity in heavy industry has increased much faster
in advanced countries than in LDC's. The difference
in productivity advances is not so wide in light industries. Therefore, again, LDC's, including Korea,
are better off with exports in light industry.

Korea's wages can be compared with Japan's wages
which can represent the wage structure of Korea's
trade partners in industrial countries. Korea's lower
wages are relatively sufficient to bring about absolute cost advantages in most industries. Money wage-
rate differences more than offset the productivity
differences, although the sampling and homogeneity
of industries are somewhat different in the two countries. Generally speaking, at the existing exchange
rates, monthly wages in Japan are four to seven times
higher than those in Korea as shown in Table 3.3,
while the productivity differences are on the average
three times higher as shown in Table 3.1.

Furthermore, in Korea, wages are relatively similar in all industries except in basic metals and a
few other industries (see Table 3.3). In Japan, on
the other hand, wages in capital-goods industries
are higher than those in consumer goods. The divergence can be explained by the need for high wages
for especially skilled workers in Japanese heavy industries. Consequently, the ratio of Japanese to
Korean wages is highest in heavy industries, such as
chemicals, machinery, and transport equipment, while
the ratio is relatively low in consumer-goods industries such as textiles and wood products.

Money wages in Korea are among the lowest in the
world. As Table 3.4 shows, average monthly wages
amount to $24.8 in Korea--about 5 percent of the com-
parable U.S. figure in 1967. Korean wages are also
much lower than Japanese wages.

TABLE 3.2

Index Numbers of Labor Productivity in World Industry

Industrial Countries	Light Industry	Heavy Industry	Food & Beverages	Textiles	Paper Products	Chemical Petroleum	Basic Metals	Metal Products
1963 = 100								
1955	78	75	80	71	77	60	84	77
1958	83	78	85	77	80	67	80	80
1960	92	89	89	88	89	81	93	90
1962	97	96	95	96	96	92	95	97
1964	105	108	105	105	107	109	111	106
1965	108	112	107	108	112	116	115	110
1966	112	117	111	116	118	125	118	116
1967	114	123	114	121	122	134	126	121
LDC's								
1955	91	70	93	88	69	75	76	64
1958	94	78	94	96	81	85	73	72
1960	100	85	98	100	90	92	92	80
1962	101	96	95	101	93	97	96	94
1964	105	105	103	109	100	102	102	108
1965	113	108	106	113	103	106	104	109
1966	115	108	113	115	103	108	105	106

Source: United Nations Statistical Yearbook, 1968, pp. 58-59.

TABLE 3.3

Average Monthly Wages in Korea and Japan by Industry Group, 1965

Industry	Korea (A)		Japan (B)		B/A
	won[a]	Dollars	yen[b]	Dollars	
Food	4,380	17.5			
Beverages	6,160	24.6	32,345	89.8	4/3
Textiles	4,160	16.6	25,068	69.6	4/2
Wood Products	5,850	23.4	27,102	75.3	3/2
Paper	5,510	22.0	37,795	104.9	4/8
Printing	6,900	27.6	47,639	132.3	4/8
Rubber	4,920	19.7	32,085	89.1	4/5
Chemicals	4,510	18.0	44,091	122.5	6/8
Petroleum	5,470	21.9	52,513	145.9	6/7
Cement & Glass	5,620	22.5	36,684	101.9	4/5
Basic Metals	7,260	29.0	49,281	136.9	4/7
Machinery	3,750	15.0	38,564	107.1	7/1
Transport Equipment	4,970	19.9	43,781	121.6	6/1

[a]The exchange rate used for korea is 250 won (W) per U.S. dollar.
[b]The exchange rate used for Japan is 360 yen (¥) per U.S. dollar.

Sources: Monthly Statistical Review (The Bank of Korea, March, 1968), pp. 74–75; Yearbook of Labor Statistics (Geneva: International Labor Office, 1967), pp. 545–46.

TABLE 3.4

Monthly Wages in Korea, Japan, and the United States[a]
(in U.S. dollars)

	United States (A)		Korea (B)		Japan (C)	
	Amount	%	Amount	% of A	Amount	% of A
1957	360.8	100	19.6	5.4	53.5	14.8
1958	371.4	100	21.3	5.7	53.3	14.4
1959	385.4	100	22.8	5.9	57.8	15.0
1960	397.8	100	23.0	5.8	62.9	15.8
1961	392.5	100	21.7	5.5	68.9	17.6
1964	445.3	100	16.8	3.3	91.9	20.6
1965	459.4	100	18.8	4.1	100.3	21.8
1966	478.7	100	20.2	4.2	112.5	23.5
1967	498.0	100	24.8	5.0	126.6	25.4

[a]Hourly earnings are multiplied by 176 (on the assumption of 8 hours per day and 22 days per month.

[b]Monthly wages in Korean won are converted into U.S. dollars at the par value applicable for each year.

[c]Monthly wages in Japanese yen are converted into U.S. dollars at the par value applicable for each year.

Sources: United Nations Statistical Yearbook, 1966, pp. 530-31 and 1968, pp. 532-33.

It is reasonable to expect that the relatively low wages are likely to continue during our projection period. In other words, the assumed, high growth rate of exports is justified on the basis of international competitiveness in world markets.

AVERAGE COSTS, SUBSIDIES, AND PROFITS
IN EXPORT PRODUCTION

Table 3.5 breaks down average costs per dollar of Korean exports, by commodity, into basic manufacturing costs and other export costs, and shows total and net won profits after adding government-export subsidies per dollar of exports. Out of 22 export commodities, 14 had positive net profits at the end of 1967, 7 items had net losses, and in 2 items exporters broke about even. The average net profits on 22 commodities were only 10 won per U.S. dollar at the exchange rate of 274 won. Excluding government subsidies, only four commodities were profitable for exporters.

Except in a few items, such as tungsten, laver, and raw silk, the profit rate was below the average rate in manufacturing which was 7.8 percent in 1967.[11] Some industries (agar-agar, woolen fabric, sweaters) which gave less than a 5 percent return on exports actually performed better if profits from domestic sales at higher prices are taken into account. Exports of radios, fish net, and clothing are aimed at earning foreign exchange even at a loss and depend entirely on export subsidies.[12]

Generally speaking, it is reasonable to say that many exporters would be operating at a loss without government subsidies. But the figures in Table 3.5 may be biased, overstating costs and understating profits. Although these commodities in the table are major export items in Korea, a sample of a few firms is too small to represent the whole export industry. The selection of appropriate export price is difficult because prices vary depending on the classification of products. Furthermore, Korean exporters are generally reluctant to reveal the true cost of exports

TABLE 3.5

Average Costs of Exports per Dollar[a] (in won)[b]

Commodity	Unit	Export Price($)[c]	Basic Costs[d]	Export Costs	Total Costs	Government Subsidies[e]	Total Profits[f]	Net Profits[g]
Fresh fish	kg.	0.62	340.11	0.77	340.88	61.40	-66.88	-5.48
Frozen shrimp	lbs.	1.40	370.13	0.21	370.35	50.35	-96.35	-48.00
Cuttle fish	st.	372.50	267.73	--	267.73	10.17	6.27	16.44
Laver	Bundle	2.32	220.64	4.27	224.91	2.10	49.09	51.19
Tobacco	kg.	0.89	268.88	2.61	335.13	5.71	-2.52	8.23
Raw silk	kg.	7.30	251.97	5.80	257.77	6.67	16.23	22.90
Tungsten	S/T	41.00	153.61	14.04	167.65	30.29	106.35	139.85
Agar-agar	lbs.	2.80	274.00	1.13	275.13	11.15	-1.13	10.02
Plywood	1,000 ft.	41.00	280.05	18.09	298.14	40.58	-24.14	16.44
Cotton fabric	yd.	0.14	400.07	9.43	409.50	109.07	-135.50	-26.43
Silk fabric	yd.	1.70	272.12	12.19	284.31	26.75	-10.31	16.40
Rayon	yd.	0.13	275.54	12.54	288.08	6.92	-14.08	7.16
Woolen	yd.	2.10	292.38	34.29	326.67	63.63	-52.67	10.96
Nylon	yd.	0.20	327.49	8.96	336.45	62.07	-62.45	-0.38
Resclellace	yd.	0.28	261.54	43.92	305.46	31.46	-31.46	0.00
Wallpaper	yd.	3.20	282.94	15.46	298.40	8.40	-24.40	-16.00
Fish net	pc.	3.25	309.53	9.37	318.90	50.59	-44.90	5.69
Shibori	ed.	0.60	288.43	24.94	313.37	53.07	-39.37	13.70
Radios	set	2.20	239.78	38.89	278.67	8.78	-4.67	4.11
Shirts	d2	7.80	290.44	15.46	305.90	37.44	-31.90	5.54
Sweaters	d2	11.50	292.44	18.98	311.42	48.22	-37.42	10.80
Wigs	pc.	17.70	292.28	10.38	302.66	2.66	-28.66	-26.00
Averages			284.19	13.72	300.79	33.10	-24.13	9.87

[a] Major export commodities at the end of 1967; [b] exchange rate used is 1 U.S. dollar = 274 won; [c] F.O.B. price; [d] manufacturing and administrative costs; [e] includes interest, tax, and other benefits; [f] excludes governmental subsidies; [g] includes governmental subsidies.

Source: *Korean Export Industry* (Seoul: Korean Trade Association, 1968), pp. 182-83.

because they fear that government subsidies may be taken away. Therefore, many exporters report higher costs for tax purposes.

NET-EXCHANGE EARNINGS FROM EXPORTS

Actually, net-exchange earnings, or foreign-currency value added, are more meaningful figures than total export proceeds to see the effect of exports on the balance of payments. Korean exports, especially of manufactures, depend on imported raw materials and intermediate goods.

As can be seen from Table 3.6, the average net-exchange earnings rate from all export commodities was in the range of 69 percent to 83 percent in 1962-66. Net-exchange earnings in secondary industry are much lower than in primary industry, which accounted for 95 percent of total net earnings from exports in 1962. However, the absolute amount of exports and the net-exchange earnings rate in secondary industry have improved in recent years.

The net-earnings rate of major manufacturing exports is shown in Table 3.7. The commodities with a net-exchange earnings rate above 50 percent are only three--clothing, wigs, and wallpaper--and accounted for only about a fifth of the total export value of manufactured goods in 1965-66.

In conclusion, it is safe to say that the rate of profits from Korean exports has been very low because of high costs as well as frequent and prevalent overvaluation of the exchange rate and that the net-exchange earnings rate has also been low because of the high imports content of exports. It is questionable whether resources are most efficiently used in export industries at the expense of alternative domestic uses. Kuznets suspects that resources have been wasted in export promotion in Korea.[13] The social costs and opportunity costs of government-export subsidies are quite high. Korean exporters have been under immense pressure to achieve export targets; in the event of failure to meet targets, the government

TABLE 3.6

Net Foreign-Exchange Earnings from Exports
(in millions of U.S. dollars)

	1962	1963	1964	1965	1966
Exports					
Primary industry	44.6	47.2	59.8	69.2	105.9
Secondary industry	12.1	38.1	55.3	103.1	142.5
Total	56.7	85.3	115.1	171.3	248.4
Net Foreign-Exchange Earnings[a]					
Primary industry	44.6	47.2	59.8	69.2	105.9
Secondary industry	2.4	16.5	19.2	49.2	68.4
Total	47.0	63.7	79.0	118.4	174.3
Net-Earnings Rate[b]					
Primary industry	19.6	43.3	34.7	47.7	48.0
Secondary industry	82.9	74.7	68.6	68.7	70.1
Total	100.0	100.0	100.0	100.0	100.0

[a]Net-exchange earnings = export-import requirements.
[b]Net-earnings rate is the ratio of net exchange earnings over the value of exports and is given in percentages.

Source: Korean Export Industry (Seoul: Korean Trade Association, 1968), pp. 195-97.

TABLE 3.7

Important Industrial Exports and Net-Exchange Earnings Rate
(in thousands of U.S. dollars)

Commodity	1965		1966		Net Earnings Rate	
	Amount	% of Total Exports	Amount	% of Total Exports	1965	1966
Plywood	18,897	11.0	30,451	12.3	28.9	24.8
Clothing	18,963	11.0	30,272	12.2	54.6	57.1
Wigs			11,740	7.4	97.0	92.3
Cotton fabric	9,428	5.5	8,304	3.3	34.1	27.9
Steel plate	11,073	6.4	8,115	3.3	40.7	35.8
Shoes	4,213	2.4	5,145	2.1	35.0	27.7
Radios	1,381	0.8	2,625	1.1	44.0	50.3
Woolen fabric	2,360	1.4	2,545	1.0	39.6	31.4
Fish net	1,223	0.7	2,139	0.9	30.8	32.2
Wallpaper	1,335	0.8	1,392	0.6	94.2	92.2
Tires	986	0.6	1,355	0.5	40.7	35.8
Rayon	1,425	0.8	1,084	0.4	26.1	36.8
Sewing machines	511	0.3	732	0.3	25.3	23.5

Source: Korean Export Industry (Seoul: Korean Trade Association, 1968), p. 197.

103

has threatened to cut off subsidies and import privileges.[14] Imports are linked to exports--imports
are allowed mainly to those who have a record of export earnings.[15] Many Korean exporters find that
losses must be taken on exports to make profits on
imports and output for the home market.

In short, Korean exporters have been making low
or negative profits, mainly because of dependence on
imported raw materials and equipment. These losses
have been offset by higher profits from import and
domestic sales. Consequently, price structures have
also distorted the domestic markets. In order to obtain the assumed growth rate of exports in our projection, the amount of government subsidies should
be raised and continued in the future.

INTERNATIONAL DEMAND

The international demand for Korean exports can
be partially analyzed by studying the geographical
and commodity composition and foreign tariffs affecting Korean exports.

Geographical Composition

As noted previously, trade between developed
countries has increased over the years more than trade
between developed countries and LDC's. The share of
developed countries' imports going to other developed
countries increased from 70 percent in 1961 to 74 percent in 1965. (See Table 3.8). LDC's are dependent
on markets in industrial countries. Developed countries have been taking about three quarters of the
LDC's exports without much change in recent years.
According to Lary, exports of light-consumer manufactures from LDC's to developed countries have increased
sharply in recent years. He suggests that the increase was possible because LDC's have a comparative
advantage in labor-intensive manufactures, and he believes that the increase can continue unless industrial countries restrict further imports from LDC's.
During 1953-65, exports of labor-intensive manufactures from LDC's to developed countries increased at

TABLE 3.8

Direction of World Exports
(in millions of U.S. dollars)

From Developed Countries to	1961 Amount	1961 Per-cent	1962 Amount	1962 Per-cent	1963 Amount	1963 Per-cent	1964 Amount	1964 Per-cent	1965 Amount	1965 Per-cent
Developed countries	63,531	69.9	69,952	71.2	75,238	72.2	86,221	72.9	95,906	74.4
LDC's	21,756	23.9	21,388	22.4	22,410	21.5	24,625	20.8	26,394	20.5
Soviet area	3,377	3.7	3,470	3.6	3,837	3.7	4,841	4.1	5,160	4.0
Unclassified	2,242	2.5	2,632	2.8	2,671	2.6	2,540	2.2	1,499	1.1
Total	90,906	100.0	95,442	100.0	104,150	100.0	118,227	100.0	128,959	100.0

From LDC's to	1961 Amount	1961 Per-cent	1962 Amount	1962 Per-cent	1963 Amount	1963 Per-cent	1964 Amount	1964 Per-cent	1965 Amount	1965 Per-cent
Developed countries	19,084	76.1	20,397	76.6	22,374	77.1	24,171	75.4	26,671	77.2
LDC's	4,705	18.8	4,871	18.3	5,132	17.7	6,033	18.8	5,606	16.9
Soviet area	825	3.3	898	3.4	1,069	3.7	1,380	4.3	1,596	4.8
Unclassified	469	1.8	464	1.7	450	1.5	475	1.5	387	1.1
Total	25,083	100.0	26,600	100.0	29,025	100.0	32,059	100.0	33,260	100.0

Source: Direction of Trade: Annuals 1961-65 (Washington, D.C.: International Monetary Fund and International Bank for Reconstruction and Development).

105

about 13 percent per annum compounded.[16] The potential market expansion of LDC exports exists mainly
in developed countries because many developing countries restrict the import of consumer goods from
other LDC's.

What then is the geographical composition of
Korean exports? After the Korean War, exports to all
countries began to increase and so did geographical
diversification. A major expansion came about during
the first-plan period. The number of countries who
import Korean goods increased from about 30 in 1960
to 64 in 1966. Nevertheless, geographical concentra-
tion remains high.

Asia and North America are the two major purchasers of Korean goods, sharing 89 percent of total
exports, and Japan and the United States alone account for 74 percent of Korean sales (Table 3.9).
However, the share of Asian countries has declined
substantially over the years. The share of the United
States, on the other hand, has increased greatly since
1962.

The relative importance of manufactured exports
to Japan has increased substantially as Korea has expanded its industrial production. The ratio of manufactures to total exports has increased from 4.5
percent in 1962 to 11.5 percent in 1966.[17] The values
of export commodities exceeding $1 million are listed
in Table 3.10.

Exports to the United States have become a source
of rapid growth of Korean foreign-exchange earnings
in the 1960's; they did in fact grow at 61 percent
annually in 1962-68. As Table 3.11 shows, the major
export commodities to the United States are manufactured goods, including plywood, cotton, woolens,
clothing, shoes, and wigs. Exports to Europe, South
America, and Africa are still negligible.

In conclusion, then, as Lary has suggested, the
LDC's have hardly scratched the surface of the market
for many light manufactures in industrial countries,
particularly in the high cost U.S. market, but much

TABLE 3.9

Geographical Composition of Korean Exports
(in thousands of U.S. dollars)

	1962		1964		1965		1966		1968	
	Amount	Per-cent	Amount	Per-cent	Amount	Per-cent	Amount	Per-cent	Amount	Per-cent
(1) Asia	37,487	66.1	66,026	55.5	85,757	49.0	104,836	41.9	151,944	33.4
Japan	(26,411)	(46.6)	(38,158)	(32.0)	(43,974)	(25.1)	(66,293)	(26.5)	(99,744)	(21.9)
(2) North America	14,118	24.9	36,253	30.4	64,463	36.8	102,055	40.8	250,943	55.1
United States	(13,993)	(24.7)	(35,566)	(29.9)	(61,695)	(35.2)	(95,789)	(38.3)	(235,402)	(51.7)
(3) Europe	4,844	8.5	15,716	13.2	21,397	12.2	34,148	13.6	36,272	8.0
(4) South America	--	--	60	0.1	132	0.1	369	0.1	125	0.1
(5) Africa	67	0.1	321	0.3	2,086	1.2	7,017	2.8	12,293	2.7
(6) Oceania	182	0.3	657	0.5	1,247	0.7	1,907	0.7	3,751	0.8
(7) Other	55	0.1	25	--	--	--	3	--	72	--
Total	56,701	100.0	119,058	100.0	175,082	100.0	250,334	100.0	455,401	100.0

Sources: Economic Statistics Yearbook (The Bank of Korea, 1964, 1967); Monthly Economic Statistics (The Bank of Korea, November, 1969).

108   FOREIGN CAPITAL FOR ECONOMIC DEVELOPMENT

depends on future U.S. policy.[18] Also there is a
time limit in which exports to Japan can continue un-
abated, mainly because of the limited size of Japan's
market. Therefore, Korea must penetrate other markets. The market potential exists in certain Latin
American and African countries which export raw materials and need manufactured imports. The market
potential is certainly also great in Europe which
can import cheap labor-intensive goods.

Commodity Composition

As mentioned before, the relative importance of
manufactured goods in Korean exports has increased
considerably. This means that the commodity composition of exports has moved in favor of goods having
relatively higher income and price elasticities.

TABLE 3.10

Major Export Commodities to Japan
(in thousands of U.S. dollars)

Commodity	1965	1966
Live fish	1,173	1,741
Fresh fish	5,994	4,937
Dried fish	3,421	1,165
Spiced fish	1,273	3,500
Rice	3,080	7,382
Laver	3,509	6,601
Raw silk	83	2,904
Iron ore	7,477	8,120
Amorphous graphite	1,233	2,819
Copper	765	1,832
Tungsten	480	2,252
Agar-agar	1,388	1,704
Bituminous coal	2,182	1,611
Textiles	1,747	4,495

Source: The Korean Trade Structure and Policies
(Seoul: Ministry of Finance, 1967), p. 117.

TABLE 3.11

Major Export Commodities to the United States
(in thousands of U.S. dollars)

Commodity	1965	1966
Cotton	1,797	7,905
Raw silk	6,564	9,126
Tungsten	1,311	1,784
Plywood	17,407	30,458
Cotton fabric	2,970	3,809
Woolen fabric	2,262	2,394
Radios	604	1,447
Clothing	11,998	12,593
Shoes	3,364	4,139
Wigs	1,563	10,616

Source: The Korean Trade Structure and Policies
          (Seoul: Ministry of Finance, 1967), p. 130.

Table 3.12 shows that semi-manufactured goods are the largest single commodity group exported. This group has also shown the largest increase in recent years. Among the semi-manufactures, major items are veneer sheets, plywood, and textiles. Exports of miscellaneous manufactured articles, including clothing, human hair, and wigs, have also increased sharply in recent years. By and large, the commodity structure of exports is beginning to conform to the theory that Korea should specialize in light manufactured products in which the country should have a comparative advantage.

Tariffs in Developed Countries

Raising the exports of light manufactures is not free of problems. Such products are protected through tariffs and other restrictions in developed countries. Because many developed countries still have labor-intensive manufactures, there is pressure to protect local industries.

TABLE 3.12

Composition of Exports
(in million of U.S. dollars)

SITC Code[a]	Commodities	1959	1960	1962	1964	1965	1966	No. of times increase 1959-66[b]	1967	1968
0	Food and live animals	4.1	9.7	21.8	26.4	28.2	41.3	10.0	37.9	44.5
03	Fish and fish preparations	1.2	2.7	8.3	15.2	17.8	21.7	18.1	26.9	25.8
04	Cereals and cereal preparations	0.8	3.8	9.0	2.4	3.6	7.3	9.1	.8	.8
	Rice	0.8	3.8	8.9	2.4	3.2	6.8	8.5	--	--
	Dried laver	1.2	1.3	0.7	5.5	3.3	8.7	7.3	6.5	13.7
1	Beverage and tobacco	0.1	0.5	0.1	0.2	0.9	6.9	69.0	7.0	8.6
12	Tobacco	0.1	0.3	0.1	0.2	0.9	6.5	65.0	6.7	7.8
2	Crude materials, inedible, excl. fuels	11.7	15.8	19.4	31.4	37.0	46.7	4.0	58.0	61.5
	Textile fibers (not manufactured)	1.0	1.4	4.4	7.1	7.7	12.9	12.9	17.0	20.0
	Raw silk	0.7	1.0	4.0	5.4	6.5	11.6	16.6	14.9	18.0
28	Metalliferrous ores and metal scrap	6.0	7.7	7.9	13.2	17.7	21.0	3.5	21.6	25.8
	Iron ore	2.2	2.5	3.8	6.0	6.7	6.1	2.8	6.0	7.3
	Tungsten ore	3.4	4.7	3.4	4.7	6.3	9.5	2.8	11.0	11.0
29	Crude animal and vegetable materials	2.2	3.6	3.9	6.4	6.9	7.7	3.5	10.9	9.3
	Ginseng	0.1	0.1	0.2	1.2	1.9	2.0	20.0	2.9	4.4
	Agar-agar	0.7	0.9	1.3	2.0	2.3	2.9	4.1	4.7	1.8
3	Mineral fuels	0.7	0.7	2.8	2.5	1.9	1.5	2.1	1.8	2.2
4	Animal and vegetable oils and fats	0.2	0.2	0.1	0.1	0.1	0.1	-	0.1	0.1
5	Chemicals	0.1	0.4	1.0	0.6	0.4	0.7	7.0	2.4	3.1
6	Semi-manufactured goods	2.1	3.9	6.2	42.3	66.4	84.2	40.1	101.4	143.6
63	Wood and cork	--	--	2.3	11.5	18.2	30.6	25.5	36.6	65.9
	Veneer sheets and plywoods	--	--	2.3	11.4	18.0	29.9	24.9	36.4	65.6

| | | | | | | | | No. of times increase | | |
SITC Code	Commodities	1959	1960	1962	1964	1965	1966	1959-66	1967	1968
65	Textiles	1.4	2.4	2.2	19.6	26.3	34.5	24.6	49.0	61.2
	Cotton fabrics, woven	1.4	2.4	1.8	11.1	10.5	10.1	7.2	12.6	13.3
7	Machinery and transport equipment	--	0.1	1.4	2.2	5.5	9.6	--	14.1	24.5
71	Machinery, excluding electrical	--	--	0.3	0.5	2.5	3.7	5.3	4.0	4.2
72	Electrical machinery and appliances	--	--	1.0	1.0	1.9	5.1	5.0	7.4	18.9
73	Transport equipment	--	--	1.0	0.7	1.1	0.8	4.0	2.8	1.4
8	Miscellaneous manufactured articles	0.1	0.1	2.0	13.2	34.5	59.2	59.2	97.2	167.0
84	Clothing	--	--	1.1	6.6	20.7	34.4	31.3	59.2	112.2
85	Footwear	--	--	0.2	0.9	4.1	5.5	27.5	8.1	11.0
89	Miscellaneous manufactures	--	--	0.5	5.0	8.9	18.9	27.0	27.6	40.9
	Human hair and wigs	--	--	--	3.7	6.8	15.5	77.5	23.4	34.4
9	Unclassified	--	1.9	0.1	0.2	0.2	0.2	--	.2	.2
	Total Exports	19.2	32.8	54.8	119.1	175.1	250.3	13.0	320.2	455.4

Note: (--) denotes small magnitude.

aSITC stands for the standard international trade classification by the United Nations.

bIn calculating the number of times increase in 1959-66, the figures near 1959 are used as the base year if 1959 figures are zero.

Source: Economic Statistics Yearbook (Bank of Korea, 1964-67); Monthly Economic Statistics (Bank of Korea, November, 1969).

Tariffs are a frequently employed means. Many economists believe that effective tariff rates in advanced countries are generally higher than nominal rates.[19] The effective rate rather than nominal rates is more appropriate for assessing the restrictive effect of a tariff structure on trade, because it relates tariff subsidy on output and tariff costs on material-import inputs to production processes, i.e., value added.[20] Furthermore, the effective rate is relatively high in the case of light-consumer goods, in which LDC's are likely to have an actual or potential comparative advantage. While the effective rate is relatively low in the case of raw materials and capital goods, this "escalated tariff structure" of advanced countries is a hindrance to increased exports by LDC's.

Table 3.13 shows effective and nominal tariff rates on some manufactures which are of definite interest to Korean exports. Most of the effective rates in the United States, the European Economic Community (EEC) and Japan are higher than nominal rates. Furthermore, the effective rate on value added by labor tends to be higher than the effective rate on total-value added. The difference is wide enough to be significant even if the measurements lack precision.

Besides tariff rates, quantitative restraints such as quotas or less visible barriers--administrative red tape and producers' collusion--tend to exist in developed countries.[21] Subtle ways to restrict imports of manufactured goods from LDC's are so-called voluntary restraints by the exporters. Such arrangements were agreed upon between the United States and the LDC's in the 1962 cotton-textile negotiation.[22] Moreover, the U.S. Trade Expansion Act of 1962 and the John F. Kennedy round of GATT negotiations (General Agreement on Tariffs and Trade) seem to have had as their primary concern trade among developed countries; limited attention was paid to tariff reductions for LDC's.[23]

Precisely because of such barriers against manufactures of LDC's, including Korea, UNCTAD has

TABLE 3.13

Nominal Tariff Rates and Estimated Effective Rates on Imports of Selected Products and Manufactures
(in percent)

SITC Code	Product	Nominal Tariff Rates			Est'd. Effective Rates on Value Added			Est'd. Effective Rates on Value Added by Labor		
		U.S.	EEC	Japan	U.S.	EEC	Japan	U.S.	EEC	Japan
	Intermediate Products									
6513	Cotton yarn and thread	13.1	10.0	5.6	32.8	31.4	13.9	46.0	44.0	19.5
6512	Yarn of wool and animal hair	23.0	5.7	10.0	53.2	16.1	29.6	74.5	22.5	41.5
611	Leather	9.6	7.3	19.9	25.7	18.3	59.0	48.1	34.3	110.4
243	Wood, shaped or simply worked	0.7	3.2	5.9	1.1	4.5	13.3	1.9	7.5	22.5
	Finished Manufactures									
652	Cotton fabrics, woven	17.5	15.0	10.5	31.2	27.5	20.0	43.4	38.5	27.8
6532	Woolen fabrics, woven	50.1	16.0	20.0	119.1	36.9	43.1	165.6	51.3	60.0
841	Cotton clothing	26.6	18.5	21.0	48.1	28.1	40.3	77.4	45.2	64.8
841	Wool clothing	22.1	20.5	22.0	-5.4	32.4	30.8	-8.7	52.2	49.6
8414	Clothing and accessories, knitted	25.6	18.6	26.0	48.7	41.3	60.8	68.5	58.1	85.5
6534	Jute fabrics, woven	2.8	23.0	25.0	7.0	62.2	67.5	9.9	86.6	94.0
6561	Jute sacks and bags	7.5	19.4	25.0	16.6	19.2	34.5	25.0	29.0	52.0
6556	Cordage, ropes, nets, etc.	4.0	14.3	19.2	11.3	41.9	57.2	32.7	121.8	166.4
851	Shoes	16.6	19.9	29.5	25.3	33.0	45.1	47.6	62.0	84.8
612/831	Other leather goods	15.5	14.7	23.6	24.5	24.3	33.6	34.3	34.0	47.0
6312/632	Plywood	17.1	15.0	20.0	43.7	32.5	44.2	87.5	65.0	88.4
821	Other wood products, incl. furniture	12.8	15.1	19.5	26.4	28.6	33.9	46.4	50.3	59.6

Source: Hal Lary, Imports of Manufactures from Less Developed Countries (New York: National Bureau of Economic Research, 1968), p. 120.

advocated not only tariff preferences in advanced
countries but also protective tariffs in LDC's.
UNCTAD considers such preferential tariff arrangements as critically important aspects of putting
LDC's on the path of self-supporting growth and of
overcoming difficulties in competing with the developed countries.

The argument for LDC tariff preferences in developed countries is considered to be a logical ex-
tension of the infant-industry argument.[24] Efficiency in export industries is possible through expansion
of foreign markets and economies of scale. Such tariff preferences mean "a social investment by the
consumers of the developed countries, the return on
which will accrue to the producers of the less-
developed countries, except to the extent that the
maturation of the infant industry actually has the
effect of reducing world-market prices."[25]

Tariff preferences are not the panacea for all
economic ills of LDC's. Although there is no statistical evidence, the over-all effective tariff rates
actually paid on imports from LDC's might be low if
special regional concessions are taken into account.
Commonwealth members and the associated overseas territories of the Common Market receive special preferences. Korea also receives special concessions from
the United States as an ally in the Vietnam war.
Furthermore, some of the labor-intensive manufactures
by LDC's are already competitive in world markets,
and general discriminatory preferences in favor of
LDC's are of course damaging to free trade as a worldwide objective.

In conclusion, however, Korea is on the verge of
breaking off from its poverty and backwardness through
international trade. It is quite understandable that
Korea asks for trade preferences from advanced countries. Trade concession from the United States is
only limited to goods and services destined for the
Vietnam war. The optimistic growth rate of exports
in the projection can be achieved with less difficulties if tariff preferences are to be given in the
future.

EXPORT-PROMOTION MEASURES

Special measures to promote exports have been
government policy in Korea. Broadly speaking, promotion measures before 1964 emphasized direct subsidies. Since that year, indirect incentives have been
more widely used, such as tax benefits, credit preferences, and special fluctuating-exchange rates.[26]
The objective of all these measures is ultimately
the same--to direct resources into various export
industries in response to changes in relative prices,
costs, or rates of return. Exports are expanded by
these measures because the required supply and demand elasticities are clearly present for the goods
so favored.[27]

After the Korean War, the Korean currency was
overvalued because of spiraling domestic prices. In
order to compensate exporters, an export-subsidy fund
was established in 1954. The commodities then eligible for direct subsidies numbered only five. By
the late 1950's, this number had grown to about 70.[28]
The military government sharply raised the export-
subsidy fund in 1961; it offered direct subsidies to
exporters and also provided for government absorption
of all or a proportion of ocean freight.[29] Direct
export subsidies were discontinued after several devaluations in 1964 and the establishment of a
fluctuating-exchange rate in 1965.

Tax Exemptions

Tax exemptions can be broadly classified into
two groups--domestic taxes and customs. Currently,
a tax exemption from corporate and individual income
taxes is granted on 50 percent of profits from exports. Exporters are also given complete exemptions
from the business-activity tax and the commodity tax.
Exemption from customs duties is granted for imports
that are reexported.[30]

As Table 3.14 shows, domestic tax and customs
exemptions have increased since 1963, concomitantly
with a major rise in Korean exports. The sharp increase in customs-duty exemptions reflects government

116   FOREIGN CAPITAL FOR ECONOMIC DEVELOPMENT

encouragement of reexports requiring the import of
foreign raw materials and intermediate goods.

TABLE 3.14

Tax Exemptions for Export Industry
(in millions of won)

| Year | Domestic Taxes | | Custom Duties | |
	Amount	Percent[a]	Amount	Percent[b]
1963	224.5	0.9	571.4	8.9
1964	512.1	1.8	1,196.6	14.5
1965	2,275.1	5.4	2,692.0	21.4
1966	3,884.7	5.5	5,332.6	30.2
1967	6,908.0	6.6	8,225.0	32.3

[a]Domestic tax exemptions as a percentage of total
domestic taxes collected.

[b]Custom duty exemption as percentage of total custom
duties.

Source: Korean Export Industry (Seoul: Korean Trade
Association, 1968), pp. 388–89.

These exemptions have turned out to be an effective device to promote exports. But the question remains as to how effectively these privileges have
been administered. Customs officials often waive
customs duties illegally. At a higher level, one
major weakness of public administration in Korea is
excessive subservience to political power. Big businesses, which are directly tied to the group in political power, can import generally restricted goods.

Credit Preference

Special credit privileges to exporters have
probably been the single most important measure accounting for the recent rapid rise in exports, especially since severe credit controls on other borrowings

are enforced as a part of Korea's stabilization program. Special credit privileges were conferred upon
exporters by the Montarey Board in 1961. Export
loans, as shown in Table 3.15, increased from 3 percent of total private credits outstanding in 1961 to
19 percent in 1967. Interest-rate subsidies also increased to 18 percent of total export loans in 1967.
Ninety-day export credits carry an interest rate of
6 percent as compared with the interest charge of 24
percent on regular commercial bills.

A majority of export loans consists of short-
term working-capital credits. Commercial banks provide credit in the form of 90-day loans, renewable
for up to 210 days. The cost of the interest subsidy
is ultimately borne by the Bank of Korea through the
discount mechanism.[31] Commercial banks may discount
the loans at the low rate of 3.5 percent at the central bank, provided they stay within the limit of
their over-all loan ceilings.[32]

There is little doubt that export-credit privileges have helped narrow the external gap by diverting resources from the domestic market to the export
sector and by attracting idle resources into the export sector. But in order to improve the present
system, it has been suggested that longer-term loans
to export industries should be increased. Fixed-
capital credits accounted for about 30 percent of
total export loans.[33] There is great need for long-
term financing in export industries to modernize
their plants and equipment. Moreover, many manufactured exports require a long period between the opening of a letter of credit and the receipt of export
proceeds. Consequently, long-term loans will reduce
the amount of overdue loans for which exporters must
pay higher penalty rates.

Exchange-Rate Policy

The Korean Government has used three major types
of exchange-rate policies as export-promotion measures. These are: (1) multiple-exchange rates, (2)
devaluation, and (3) fluctuating-exchange rates.
Multiple-exchange rates were discontinued following

TABLE 3.15

Export Loans and Interest Subsidies
(in millions of wons)

Year	Total Private Loans[a]	Export Loans	% of Export Loans[b]	Interest Differential	Interest Subsidy Amount[c]
1961	31,998	830	2.6	0.0	0.0
1962	45,289	1,770	3.9	4.7	83.2
1963	51,947	3,890	7.5	5.8	225.6
1964	56,981	10,000	17.6	6.0	600.0
1965	75,536	12,140	16.1	17.5	2,124.5
1966	105,378	16,560	15.7	17.5	2,898.0
1967	172,960	33,270	19.2	18.0	5,988.6

[a]Loans made to the private sector by all banking institutions.

[b]Includes short-term operating loans, medium-term facility loans, import loans for reexport, export usance, and other export promotion loans.

[c]The interest subsidy is calculated by multiplying the interest differential between regular commercial and export loans by export loans.

Sources: Economic Statistics Yearbook (The Bank of Korea, 1967), p. 53 and p. 84; Monthly Statistical Review (The Bank of Korea, March, 1968), p. 34; Korean Export Industry (Korean Trade Association, 1968), pp. 395–400.

the exchange reform of 1961 under which a single, fixed-exchange rate was established. A fluctuating-exchange rate was adopted in 1965. As will be shown in the discussion below, the fluctuating-exchange rate is not a fully free rate.

Multiple-exchange rates may include preferential or penalty buying and selling rates. Theoretically, preferential-buying rates can be applied to exports with elastic supplies and a penalty-buying rate to exports of goods in inelastic supply. High penalty-selling rates are applied to essential imports.[34] Multiple-exchange rates applied to selected exports and imports with different elasticities of supply and demand may avoid general devaluation. The well-known shortcomings of such a system include the problem of administrative classification of specific commodity groups by specific rates.[35]

The Korean Government has not used multiple-exchange rate practices for the purposes described in the preceding paragraph. Multiple rates have rather been used as a defensive measure. The official rate was applied to general transactions in private foreign trade, travel abroad, and remittances of authorized parties. As shown in Table 3.16, the counterpart-fund rate and the rate for U.N. Forces had been generally higher in terms of won per dollar than the official rate to discourage the demand for imports with foreign-aid funds and to increase won purchases by U.N. Forces. (Counterpart funds refer to the won paid into a special account by Korean importers of foreign-aid goods and agricultural-surplus commodities under U.S. PL 480.) In fact, the counterpart-fund rate happened to be a preferential selling rate and the rate for U.N. Forces a penalty buying rate, because the entire structure of rates overvalued the won.

In July, 1955, for instance, when the official rate was 18 won per dollar, the counterpart-fund rate 35 won, the rate for U.N. Forces was 51 won, and the rate for U.S.-dollar notes was 90 won per dollar in the curb market (illegal or black market). Again in February, 1960, when the official rate was 65,

TABLE 3.16

Exchange Rates of Won in Relation to U.S. Dollars

Year		Official Rate Buying & Selling Rate[b]	Counter-part-Fund Rate Selling Rate	U.N. Forces[a] Buying Rate	Other U.N.-Won Transactions Buying Rate
1951	3-11	2.50	4.00	6.0	6.0
	5-1	2.50	6.00	6.0	6.0
	11-12	6.00	6.00	6.0	6.0
1953	6-1	6.00	6.00	18.0	18.0
	8-23	6.00	18.00	18.0	18.0
	12-13	18.00	18.00	18.0	18.0
1954	11-10	18.00	18.00	50.0	18.0
	11-15	18.00	15.00	50.00	31.0
1955	1-10	18.00	35.00	43.00	43.0
	2-1	18.00	35.00	50.0	50.0
	5-2	18.00	35.00	50.0	41.0
	6-6	18.00	35.00	48.0	48.0
	7-11	18.00	35.00	51.00	51.0
	8-15	30.00	30.00	50.0	50.0
1960	1-20	50.00	65.00	50.0	50.0
	2-23	65.00	65.00	65.0	65.0
1961	1-1	100.00	100.00	100.0	100.0
	2-2	130.00	130.00	130.0	130.0

[a] Prior to October 1, 1950, the rate for U.N. Forces was the same as the official rate.

[b] Buying and selling rates are those of the Bank of Korea.

Source: Economic Statistics Yearbook (The Bank of Korea, 1962), p. 198.

the curb-market rate was 145. The average curb-
market rates are shown in Table 3.17. The Rhee Government always resisted IMF and USOM (U.S. Overseas
Mission-AID) insistence on devaluation. This position was defended by stating that a majority of
Korean imports was financed by foreign aid and that
devaluation would raise the general price level. In
fact, the so-called dollar millionaires during the
Rhee Regime were those who obtained dollars at the
low official rate, sold imported goods at high domestic prices, and made windfall profits. The over-
hauled exchange rate of course also discouraged exports.

In 1964, for the first time, the official and
curb-market rates moved close to each other. The
official and curb-market rates clustered around 270
in 1965-66. Then the gap between the two rates
started to widen again as domestic prices increased
substantially.

TABLE 3.17

Monthly Average Curb-Market Exchange Rates
(in won per U.S. dollar)

	Date	Rate		Date	Rate
1955	July	90	1960	October	126
1959	October	124		November	126
	November	128		December	133
	December	130	1961	January	141
1960	January	137		February	150
	February	145	1962	October	155
	March	143	1963	March	160
	April	147	1964	May	260
	May	153	1965	December	272
	June	141	1966	December	275
	July	142	1967	December	290
	August	126	1968	December	300
	September	123	1969	December	320

Sources: IMF Consultation Mission (Seoul: The Bank
of Korea, 1962), p. 101; interviews with
officials of the Bank of Korea in New York
City.

Usually, the purpose of general devaluation is
to improve the balance of payments by raising exchange proceeds from exports and lowering exchange
payments for imports. Such at least will be the case
given certain supply-and-demand elasticities. By
raising domestic prices of exports and imports, devaluation draws resources into both export- and
import-substituting industries. In short, a devaluation is recommended only when the balance of payments
is in fundamental disequilibrium.[36]

There have been seven devaluations in Korea
since 1953. Korean devaluations did not play an active role in stimulating exports; rather, they played
a passive role of offsetting the negative-competitive
effect on exports of domestic inflation. The devaluations have broadly followed domestic-price increases,
as illustrated in Table 3.18. Devaluations tended to
be larger when domestic prices had shown greater percentage increases, and they were less after periods
of relative price stability. Basically, then, the exchange rate has reflected purchasing-power parity
considerations.[37]

Technically, exchange-rate changes after 1965
are not devaluations but depreciations. A free-
exchange certificate market was established in March,
1965. Theoretically, the rate of the won is allowed
to fluctuate in response to market forces. But it
is still far from a truly free rate. First, domestic
residents who earned or received foreign exchange are
supposed to surrender it and receive Korean won or,
alternatively, foreign-exchange certificates. These
certificates can be sold in the market within 30 days
after they are obtained. Second, the Bank of Korea
has participated in the market to maintain the stability of the rate when the exchange rate moved above
or below 1 percent of the basic, official rate. Finally, the fluctuating rate is not really a reflec-
tion of free demand and supply in the market because
the actual uses of foreign exchange are restricted
by trade and exchange controls.

Although the present exchange rate is still far
from an equilibrium rate, it is the closest to a free

TABLE 3.18

Devaluations, Wholesale- and Consumer-Price Changes
(percentage of change)

Effective Date	Official Rate[a]	Devaluation Percentage[b]	Wholesale Prices[c]	Consumer Prices[c]
1951, November 10	6.0	--	--	--
1953, December 15	18.0	200.0	159.6	205.7
1955, August 15	50.0	177.8	141.9	154.1
1960, February 23	65.0	30.0	56.4	58.6
1961, January 1	100.0	53.9	10.9	10.8
February 2	130.0	30.0	4.9	2.4
1964, May 3	255.0	96.2	87.8	76.9
1965, December 31	272.0	6.9	6.4	8.3
1966, December 31	272.0	0.0	8.1	16.5
1967, December 31	274.6	1.0	7.4	10.8
1968, December 31	281.5	2.5	7.1	10.9
1969, September 30	288.8	2.5	5.4	6.2

[a] won per U.S. dollar.

[b] Calculated as follows: new rate = (won per U.S. dollar) ÷ previous rate (won per U.S. dollar).

[c] The base year in subperiods is as follows: 1947 = 100 in 1951-54, 1955 = 100 in 1955-59, 1960 = 100 in 1960-66, and 1965 = 100 in 1967. In the calculations, an annual average is used instead of a monthly average when the latter is exceptionally high.

Sources: Economic Statistics Yearbook (The Bank of Korea, 1955, 1960); Price Statistics Summary (The Bank of Korea, 1966); Monthly Statistical Review (The Bank of Korea, March, 1968 and November, 1969).

rate Korea has ever had. As mentioned before, both
official and curb-market rates stayed around 270 won
per dollar until recently. It may be safe to conclude
that the devaluations of 1964 and the exchange reform
of 1965 helped the rise of exports in recent years,
even after taking into account the heavy import content of exports. However, the official exchange rate
has tended to become unrealistic again. The official
exchange rate has stayed relatively constant while
wholesale prices have increased by more than 40 percent since 1965. Consequently, the curb-market rate
has recently reached approximately 320.

At the Joint Economic Meeting between Korea and
the United States in June, 1968, USOM suggested a
depreciation of the exchange rate to 300. But the
Korean Government refused to do so, arguing that the
depreciation would increase the general price level
rather than exports because of the high import content of exports and because Korean demand is rather
inelastic. The Korean Government further argued that
the depreciation would raise the burden of external-
debt service.[38]

Many Korean exporters are operating at a loss,
even with the help of government subsidies which now
amount to 33 won per dollar of exports' proceeds.
The average net profits on major export items are
only 10 won per dollar, or about 3 percent of the won
price.

Either the overvalued exchange rate or export
subsidies will eventually have to be readjusted.
Exchange-rate depreciation is to be preferred. A
truly free exchange rate would reflect impersonal
market decisions while administrative difficulties
are associated with government subsidies.

The adverse effects of an overvalued exchange
rate are numerous. Exporters are not inclined to
export goods at low rates of return. An overvalued
rate may raise the prices of Korean goods for foreign
importers, and Korean goods thus may not be competitive in the world market. Also, overvaluation has
unfavorable effects on the inflow of foreign capital.

Naturally, one possible solution would be for Korea
to adopt stabilization measures and enforce equilibrium at the present exchange rate or to do so after
one more devaluation.[39]

In summary, while Korean competitiveness at the
prevailing exchange rates appears to have been favorable, government stimulus to exports--including exchange practices, devaluations, and subsidies--helped
achieve the high, observed growth rate. Also the
favorable performance of Korean exports in her traditional markets in the United States and Japan was
compatible with the high growth rate. Finally, the
rapid industrialization efforts have enhanced the
commodity composition of exports which are greatly
demanded in advanced countries.

However, there still remains room for further
improvements in government-export promotion measures
such as the establishment of realistic exchange rates
and effective subsidy administration. Bottlenecks
to the supply of exports can be eliminated through
interindustry coordinations. Market researches to
explore new foreign markets are also desired through
international cooperation. Then, the over-all growth
rate in the projection seems plausible.

NOTES

1.   See Ragner Nurske, Patterns of Trade and
Development (Oxford: Basil Blackwell, 1961), p. 15.

2.   John Pincus, Trade, Aid, and Development
(New York: McGraw-Hill, 1967), p. 58.

3.   Nurske, op. cit., p. 23.

4.   R. Prebisch, "Commercial Policy in the Under-
developed Countries," The American Economic Review
(May, 1959), pp. 251-73; and R. Prebisch, "Towards A
New Trade Policy for Development," Proceedings of
UNCTAD (New York: United Nations, 1964), pp. 10-11.

5. Charles P. Kindleberger, Foreign Trade and the National Economy (New Haven: Yale University Press, 1962), pp. 102-13.

6. H. W. Singer, International Development (New York: McGraw-Hill, 1964), pp. 165-66.

7. Prebisch, "Towards a New Trade Policy," op. cit., pp. 21-23.

8. Industrialization and Foreign Trade (League of Nations, 1945), p. 116.

9. Nurske, op. cit., p. 37.

10. Donald MacDougal, "British and American Exports: A Study Suggested by the Theory of Comparative Costs," Economic Journal (December, 1951), pp. 697-724; Bela Balassa, "An Empirical Demonstration of the Classical Comparative Cost Theory," Review of Economics and Statistics (August, 1963), pp. 231-38.

11. Korean Export Industry (Seoul: Korean Trade Association, 1968), p. 183.

12. Ibid., pp. 181-91.

13. P. W. Kuznets, "Korea's Five-Year Plans" (Mimeographed; paper presented at the Conference on Korean Planning, Northwestern University, June 19-21, 1968), pp. 50-54.

14. Ibid.

15. Monthly Statistical Review (Seoul: Bank of Korea, February, 1965), p. 27.

16. Hal Lary, Imports of Manufactures from Less Developed Countries (New York: National Bureau of Economic Research, 1968), pp. 107-9.

17. Korean Trade Structure and Policies (Seoul: Ministry of Finance, 1967), p. 116.

18. Lary, op. cit., p. 114.

19. For instance, Bela Balassa, "Tariff P
tion in Industrial Countries: An Evaluation," Journa
of Political Economy (December, 1965), pp. 9-29;
Harry Johnson, Economic Policies Toward Less Developed
Countries (Washington, D.C.: The Brookings Institution,
1967), pp. 17-180; W. H. Corden, "The Structure of a
Tariff System and the Effective Protective Rate,"
Journal of Political Economy (June, 1966), pp. 221-37.

20. H. Burgard, "External Impact on Economic
Development," Kyklos, Vol. XX (1967), Fasc. 4, pp.
886-906.

21. Lary, op. cit., p. 122.

22. Ibid., p. 124.

23. Ibid., pp. 129-34.

24. Johnson, op. cit., p. 181.

25. Ibid.

26. A chronology of export-promotion measures
can be derived from the Monthly Statistical Review,
op. cit., from 1961 to 1968.

27. Peggy Musgrave, Trade Targets and Policies
in Korea's Economic Development (Seoul: Economic
Planning Board, 1965), pp. 18-23.

28. Balance of Payments of Korea (Seoul: Bank
of Korea, 1967), pp. 75-76.

29. Monthly Statistical Review, op. cit.,
April, 1963, p. 30; October, 1963, p. 45; and November,
1964, p. 34.

30. A Study on Legal Entity Tax in Korea (Seoul:
Korean Economic Development Institute, 1966), p. 77.

31. Review of Korean Economy, 1968 (Seoul: Bank
of Korea, 1969), pp. 124-25; Musgrave, op. cit., p. 31.

32. Ibid.

33. Korean Export Industry, op. cit., p. 396.

34. F. Mikesell, Foreign Exchange in the Post-war World (New York: The Twentieth Century Fund, 1954), p. 167.

35. Francis Schott, The Evolution of Latin American Exchange Rate Policies Since World War II (Princeton, N.J.: Department of Economics, Princeton University, 1959), pp. 7-14; and E. Schlesinger, Multiple Exchange Rates and Economic Development (Princeton, N.J.: Department of Economics, Princeton University, 1952), pp. 9-76.

36. Ragner Nurske, "Conditions of International Equilibrium," in H. S. Ellis and L. A. Metzler, eds., Readings in the Theory of International Trade (Philadelphia: The Blakiston Co., 1949), pp. 3-34.

37. Charles P. Kindleberger, International Economics (Homewood, Ill.: Richard D. Irwin, Inc., 1963), p. 76.

38. Hankook Ilbo (Korean daily newspaper; Seoul), June 23, 1968.

39. E. Sohmen, Flexible Exchange Rates (Chicago: University of Chicago Press, 1961), pp. 103-21.

CHAPTER **4** FACTORS AFFECTING
IMPORTS

INTRODUCTION

As discussed in Chapters 1 and 2, imports and
GNP are considered interdependent. In order to reach
the target GNP, a certain amount of imports is required; and a high level of GNP in turn stimulates
imports and a high import-GNP ratio until import substitution becomes an important factor in lowering the
ratio. But the relationship between imports and GNP
has been affected to a large extent by government
policy relating to quantitative restrictions and protective tariffs.

There are many factors increasing or decreasing
the import-GNP ratio. The changes in import-GNP
ratios in Korea have been strongly influenced by two
opposing forces, namely the income-creation and
import-substitution effects. The size of the external gap will increase or decrease, depending on the
assumption of the import-GNP ratio in our projection.
In this chapter, those forces affecting imports are
discussed in detail and depth.

The classical theory of free trade in its strict
sense is not applicable in the case of Korean imports.
The conventional theory is primarily concerned with
the allocation of a fixed quantity of resources which
will optimize the real income of a country. Imports
should take place if they are relatively more advantageous in terms of real-commodity prices and
underlying-cost differences than commodities produced
domestically. In the case of Korea, however, imports
are permitted not because they are comparatively advantageous but because certain imports which cannot
be supplied domestically are required in the process
of industrialization. Industrialization through

import substitution may be equally as important as
export expansion in the five-year plans, but import
substitution is not always an efficient investment,
at least in the early period of industrialization,
and is more dictated by its impact on the supply of
resources (capital) than by its effect on the allocation of existing ones. Furthermore, import substitutions usually accompany quantitative- and protective-
tariff restrictions.

The import ratio in Korea has fluctuated over
the years. The highest import ratio during the 1954-
56 period was 24.5 percent of GNP in 1957 when foreign aid also reached its peak; the ratio declined
to 15.1 percent in 1961 as foreign aid declined. The
import ratio again increased to 22 percent in 1963
when the import of investment goods and raw materials
was required for rapid industrialization. The high
ratio in 1966 is related to the high level of income
and the effect of a "negative system" which allowed
a large number of items to be imported without quantitative restrictions. Although quantitative restrictions have been liberalized to a great extent, tariff
rates are extremely high for the protection of import-
substitute industries.

COMMODITY AND GEOGRAPHICAL COMPOSITION

The commodity and geographical composition of
Korean imports reflects the vital importance of these
goods for industrialization.

Commodity Composition

In the case of Korea, the shares of primary- and
manufactured-goods imports were about equal in the
1950's. In spite of rapid industrialization since
1962, the share of manufactured imports has tended to
increase (see Table 4.1). Korea depends on imported
capital goods and industrial, crude materials because
the country is poorly endowed with natural resources,
except perhaps fishery. It must import most of the
oil, iron, and steel it needs. Korea is also dependent on foreign sources of supply for industrial

machinery and equipment. In view of the country's weak natural-resources base, one would expect Korea to import most of its raw materials and capital goods.

As Table 4.1 shows, imports have increased from $321 million in 1959-61 to $1,224.6 million in 1967-68, a compound rate of increase of 17 percent per annum. The bulk of the increase in imports has been in industrial crude materials, semiprocessed for industry. Of the total increase of $903.6 million in imports between 1959 and 1968, $385 million is represented by fuel and industrial crude materials (SITC 2-5), nearly $170 million by intermediate goods (SITC 6)--mainly partially processed items such as iron, steel, nonferrous metals, and fibers--and about $379 million by machinery and transport equipment (SITC 7).[1]

These extraordinary increases in industrial materials, semiprocessed goods, machinery, and equipment are, of course, related to the expansion of industrial production in recent years. By far the largest part of the increase in crude materials seems directly attributable to manufacturing growth such as has taken place in plywood, textiles, fertilizers, petroleum, cement, plastics, and nylon. However, to some extent, crude-materials imports (structural steel and aluminum) are also related to construction and transport activities.[2] Furthermore, the accelerated increase in investment would not have been possible without the import of capital goods. Machinery and equipment imports have been rising even faster than industrial crude materials.

The relative importance of food and fertilizer in total imports has declined substantially from 25 percent of total imports in 1959-61 to 14 percent in 1967-68. Imports of food increased in 1963, however, because of crop failures in 1962 and increased assistance under PL 480 which provided products such as barley and wheat.[3]

Geographical Composition

As Table 4.2 shows, the bulk of Korea's imports comes from the United States and Japan. Imports from

TABLE 4.1

Composition of Imports
(in millions of U.S. dollars)

SITC Code[a]	Commodities	1959-61 Amount	Percent	1962-64 Amount	Percent	1965-66 Amount	Percent	1967-68 Amount	Percent
0	Food	33.0	10.3	79.1	17.1	135.9	11.5	130.8	10.6
04	Cereals and cereal preparations	27.7	8.6	69.4	15.0	57.8	9.8	102.5	8.3
	Wheat	19.3	6.0	43.1	9.3	38.2	6.5	54.5	4.4
06	Sugar and sugar preparations	8.3	2.6	4.3	0.9	5.4	0.9	11.0	0.9
1	Beverages and tobacco	--	--	0.2	--	0.3	--	1.1	--
2	Crude material, inedible (excluding fuels)	64.7	20.2	98.0	21.2	131.9	22.4	237.8	19.3
23	Crude rubber (incl. synthetic)	6.7	2.1	6.9	1.4	8.9	1.5	6.0	0.5
24	Wood, lumber, and cork	7.3	2.3	19.7	4.3	34.7	5.9	75.0	6.1
25	Pulp and paper	3.7	1.1	9.1	1.9	11.1	1.9	19.6	1.6
26	Textile fiber (not manufactured)	44.1	13.7	53.1	11.5	63.2	10.3	85.3	6.9
	Raw cotton	29.6	9.2	36.7	7.9	41.8	7.1	49.2	4.0
27	Crude fertilizer and crude minerals	0.5	--	3.1	0.6	4.9	0.8	14.3	1.2
28	Metallic ores and metal scrap	--	--	3.4	0.6	9.2	1.5	24.1	1.9
3	Mineral fuels, lubricants, and related materials	29.5	9.2	31.2	6.7	36.9	6.2	68.5	5.6
33	Petroleum and petroleum products	24.9	7.8	28.8	6.2	34.7	5.9	66.1	5.4
4	Animal and vegetable oils and fats	3.0	0.9	4.2	0.9	4.7	0.8	15.2	0.6
5	Chemical	68.8	21.4	86.1	18.6	118.9	20.1	241.5	9.8
51	Chemical elements and compounds	5.1	1.6	12.9	2.8	18.5	3.1	40.3	3.3
53	Dyeing, tanning, and coloring materials	3.7	1.1	11.2	2.8	4.7	0.8	7.9	0.6

SITC Code	Commodities	1959-61 Amount	Percent	1962-64 Amount	Percent	1965-66 Amount	Percent	1967-68 Amount	Percent
54	Medicinal and pharmaceutical products	4.2	1.3	4.7	1.0	5.5	0.9	9.7	0.8
56	Fertilizers, manufactured	47.9	14.9	55.4	12.0	77.4	13.1	37.8	3.1
58	Plastic materials	3.4	1.1	4.5	0.9	7.2	1.2	18.5	1.1
6	Manufactured goods	41.5	12.9	69.2	15.0	98.2	16.6	212.9	17.3
65	Textile yarn fabrics	17.6	5.5	26.0	5.6	36.1	6.1	86.2	7.0
66	Nonmetallic mineral manufactures	1.8	0.5	3.6	0.6	3.8	0.6	10.9	0.9
67	Iron and steel	9.4	2.9	23.0	5.0	32.1	5.4	62.7	5.1
68	Nonferrous metals	3.3	1.0	6.8	1.4	10.1	1.7	14.2	1.1
	Aluminum	1.9	0.6	3.2	0.6	5.1	0.8	8.1	0.6
69	Manufacture of metal	2.0	0.6	5.2	1.1	12.9	2.2	30.5	2.5
7	Machinery, transport equipment	41.4	12.9	85.0	18.4	172.4	29.2	421.6	34.3
71	Machinery (except electrical)	25.4	7.9	44.9	9.7	65.4	11.1	212.1	17.2
72	Electrical machinery	12.8	4.0	23.6	5.1	19.3	3.3	71.6	5.8
73	Transport equipment	3.2	1.0	16.5	3.6	37.6	6.3	137.9	11.2
8	Miscellaneous manufactured articles	6.0	1.9	7.8	1.7	8.7	1.5	28.0	2.3
86	Professional, scientific instruments	3.8	1.2	4.6	0.9	4.7	0.8	12.1	0.9
9	Not classified	33.1	10.3	1.3	0.3	0.1	--	0.3	--
	Total imports	321.0	100.0	462.1	100.0	589.9	100.0	1,224.6	100.0

Note: (--) denotes small magnitude.

aPrimary products are defined as SITC 0-4 categories and manufactured goods as SITC 5-9.

Sources: Economic Statistics Yearbook (The Bank of Korea, 1964, 1965, 1967, 1969).

133

other countries have increased since 1962 as a result
of trade expansion programs in the First Five-Year
Economic Plan.

The relative share of imports from the United
States declined from 44 percent in 1959-61 to 32 percent in 1967-68, a decrease partially explained by
declining U.S. aid. The relative share of imports
from Japan, on the other hand, increased from 18 percent in 1959-61 to 46 percent in 1967-68. Among
other countries, only Taiwan, Hong Kong, and West
Germany represent significant shares of Korean imports.

Imports from the United States and Japan consist
mainly of industrial equipment and raw materials.
Some of the important individual items are textile
machines, electric and transport equipment, and chemical compounds.[4]

IMPORT SUBSTITUTION

Import substitution is an important factor affecting imports. On the one hand, it requires the
import of capital goods and raw materials to accel-
erate industrialization; on the other hand, it will
reduce the import-GNP ratio in the long run. Only
when the domestic supply of import substitutes is
large enough to offset the growing demand for imports
will the import-GNP ratio tend to decrease. The potential trade gap could be appreciably narrowed if
import substitution were to be successful. But the
problem of narrowing and closing the external gap
must of course be attacked simultaneously on both
fronts--export expansion and import substitution.

In the process of industrialization, newly in-
troduced or expanded products take the place of
imported goods.[5] But industrialization requires capital goods which often cannot be produced in developing countries. Therefore, the main objective of import substitution is not to reduce the level of
imports, at least in the early stage of industrialization, but to save foreign exchange, the "shadow"

TABLE 4.2

Geographical Composition of Korean Imports
(in millions of U.S. dollars)

	1959-61 Amount	1959-61 Percent	1962-64 Amount	1962-64 Percent	1965-66 Amount	1965-66 Percent	1967-68 Amount	1967-68 Percent
(1) Asia	82.2	25.6	165.4	35.8	306.5	51.9	698.5	59.7
Japan	(141.6)	(17.8)	(126.2)	(27.3)	(230.2)	(39.0)	(533.5)	(45.6)
(2) North America	146.5	45.6	240.0	51.9	221.2	37.5	389.6	33.3
United States	(141.6)	(44.1)	(235.4)	(50.9)	(218.0)	(37.0)	(377.1)	(32.2)
(3) Europe	66.3	20.6	40.8	8.8	48.2	8.2	118.8	10.2
(4) South America	4.0	1.2	1.4	0.3	1.9	0.3	3.7	0.3
(5) Africa	0.5	0.3	1.3	0.3	5.6	0.9	5.1	0.4
(6) Oceania	7.3	2.3	9.7	2.1	6.2	1.1	12.7	1.1
(7) Other	14.2	4.4	3.6	0.8	0.4	--	1.3	--
Total	321.0	100.0	462.2	100.0	589.9	100.0	1,170.2	100.0

Sources: Economic Statistics Yearbook (The Bank of Korea, 1965, 1967); Monthly Economic Statistics (The Bank of Korea, November, 1969).

price of which may be much higher than the frequently overvalued official exchange rate would indicate.

Domestic production replacing foreign "noninput" imports, which refer to nonessential consumer goods, will conserve foreign exchange for "input" imports of capital equipment.[6] The establishment of certain import-competing industries on a large scale adds to existing external economies and may pave the way for many new lines of productive activities through "backward and forward linkages" with other industries.[7] Import substitution may also promote the growth of technical skills among workers and encourage improved organization and management among entrepreneurs.[8]

Import substitution, on the other hand, may not be especially successful if there is low productivity in the consumer-goods industries and if the imported inputs needed for import-substituting goods is high. Because production costs even of consumer goods are often high in LDC's, protective tariffs are usually imposed on the basis of the infant-industry argument. In measuring the success of import substitution, both the foreign-exchange saving and the increased-value added of import substitutes are therefore appropriate criteria.

Measuring Import Substitution

The criteria mentioned above do not yield a clear-cut measurement for Korea. In static analysis, any increase in the domestic production of import substitutes would reflect import substitution. But in a constantly changing economy, if domestic production of a certain commodity increases but falls short of the growth in domestic demand for that commodity, imports will continue to rise.[9] Furthermore, total imports may increase owing to forces other than import substitution or its absence--income, prices, and tastes for foreign goods.

According to the Leff and Netto study, import substitution was not successful in Brazil, because the income-creation effect on increased imports heavily outweighed the import-substitution effect.[10]

Humphrey, on the other hand, concluded that the effect of import substitution was positive in Brazil
by comparing the import-substitute output with the
absorptive capacity of the domestic market, which
gave some idea of the growth of total importable demand. He actually used the increase in industrial
production as a proxy for the absorptive capacity.[11]
Even in product-by-product analysis, the substitution
of domestic output for an import product may create
new demands for other import products through interindustry relations.

When we consider the complexities involved in
measuring the effect of import substitution, it becomes apparent that to take the ratio of import-
substitute production to total supply of any commodity is thus only a first approximation. Nevertheless,
Table 4.3 indicates that import substitution of selected products has apparently been quite successful.
In all cases given in the table, import-substitute
production as a percentage of total supply has increased from 1957 to 1964. In the case of woolen
fabrics, 100-percent import substitution was achieved.
Such a favorable effect has been possible in part because domestic markets already existed for the products included in the table.[12] Some of the products
included, such as cement, woolen fabric, plate glass,
sugar, and radios, are now being exported.

The absolute increase in import-substitute production may be meaningless in terms of total imports,
as noted previously. In the initial period of industrialization, large amounts of imported capital goods
are needed. Yet, the important factor in the long
run in Korea is foreign-exchange saving rather than
the decrease in the level of total imports as such.
One way of measuring foreign-exchange saving is to
find the domestic-value added through import substitutes. In other words, the saving can be the value
of import substitutes, which would have been imported
without import substitution, less the value of imported inputs required to produce import substitutes domestically. On the basis of this estimate, as shown
in Table 4.4, the rate of foreign-exchange saving
ranges between 21 percent in sugar and 100 percent in

TABLE 4.3

Effect of Import Substitution
(1957 and 1964)[a]

Commodity	Unit	Imports		Production		Production as % of total supply[b]		Exports	
		1957	1964	1957	1964	1957	1964	1957	1964
Cement	m/t[c] (000)	193	28	91	1,419	32.0	98.1	0	22
Woolen fabric	ma[d] (000)	558	0	4,634	7,914	89.3	100.0	0	100
Plate glass	m/t	15,520	234	322	23,815	20.3	99.0	0	50
Sugar	m/t	2,973	0	17,087	30,820	91.2	100.0	–	4,286
Chemical fertilizers	m/t (000)	772	976	0	132	0.0	11.9	–	–
Petroleum products	m/t (000)	784	404	0	657	0.0	61.9	–	–
Paper	m/t (000)	25	12	33	104	56.9	89.7	–	–
Dyes	m/t	720	356	381	819	34.6	69.7	–	–
Radios	(000)	68	0	0	187	0.0	100.0	n.a.[e]	96
Diesel engines	m/t	253	1,205	0	1,428	0.0	54.2	–	–

Note: (–) indicates negligible amount.
[a] Figures near 1957 and 1964 if unavailable for these two years.
[b] Total supply refers to domestic production plus imports.
[c] Metric ton.
[d] Korean standard of square feet.
[e] Not available.

Sources: The Analysis on Substitute Effect of Import Substitute Industry (Korea Productivity Center, 1965); Economic Statistics Yearbook (Bank of Korea), 1967.

138

condensed milk. It may be a wise device for the government to encourage those import substitutes which
contain a high rate of foreign-exchange saving in the
present situation.

The real foreign-exchange saving may be somewhat
lower than those shown in Table 4.4, because the latter ignores the import content of capital and intermediate goods. Many economists specify, at least in
conceptual framework, investment constraint as another
factor affecting import substitution.[13] In calculating the foreign-exchange saving, the Korean Productivity Center deducted the value of imported raw materials from the unit value of import substitutes.
Unless the investment project for import substitution
has already been written off or recovered, and unless
the import content of complementary goods such as
packaging is minimal, the foreign-exchange saving is
overstated.[14]

Furthermore, for a particular import-substitution
project to be considered efficient, it must be a net
saver of foreign exchange over its lifetime as a whole.
As long as the rate of investment and the incremental
capital-output ratio remains constant, the direct impact of this year's investment on the demand for imports would be more than offset by previous years'
investments in the import-substituting industry now
coming to fruition.[15] To put the argument differently, the demand for imported capital and consumer
goods will decline as industrialization proceeds with
import substitution. A numerical illustration, demon-
strating the possible effect of import substitution
on the balance of payments through time, is given in
Table 4.5

In conclusion, it is quite difficult to measure
the true effect of import substitution. But, with
the observed facts on import substitution in Korea,
it is reasonable to conclude that many import items
have been replaced by domestic production and that
the foreign-exchange saving from import substitution
has been used for the import of capital goods and
industrial raw materials. Further, the present heavy
investment in import-substitute industries will bring

TABLE 4.4

Foreign-Exchange Saving of Import Substitutes
(in U.S. dollars as of 1964)

Commodity	Unit[a]	Unit Sales Price[b]	Imported Inputs[c]	Foreign Exchange Savings	Foreign Exchange Savings Rate
Condensed milk	can	0.34	—	0.34	100.0
Gas compressors	no.	1,960.79	—	1,960.79	100.0
PVC[d]	m/t	330.08	7.61	322.47	97.7
Sensitive paper	dozen	0.39	0.04	0.37	89.3
Urea fertilizer	m/t	58.66	6.91	51.75	88.2
Pulp	m/t	150.00	17.69	132.04	88.1
Plate glass	c/s	7.12	1.00	6.12	85.9
Passenger trains	no.	29,569.00	4,823.26	24,772.74	83.7
Portland cement	m/t	16.20	2.68	13.52	83.5
Rayon yarn	lbs.	0.46	0.11	0.35	82.6
Radios	no.	14.90	3.52	11.38	76.4
Bearings	no.	109.80	30.12	70.68	72.7
Diesel engines	no.	61.84	17.38	44.46	71.9
Caustic soda	m/t	60.30	20.76	39.60	65.6
Sewing machines	no.	34.00	11.77	22.23	65.4
Telephones	no.	17.65	6.50	11.15	63.2
Steel bars	m/t	86.27	32.81	53.64	61.9

140

Commodity	Unit[a]	Unit Sales Price[b]	Imported Inputs[c]	Foreign Exchange Savings	Foreign Exchange Savings Rate
Dyes	m/t	1,862.74	735.37	1,137.34	61.7
Nylon yarn	lbs.	1.45	0.61	0.84	54.8
Newspaper paper	m/t	107.00	51.31	55.69	52.0
Pianos	no.	426.63	210.70	215.93	50.6
Fireproof tile	m/t	20.70	10.31	10.39	50.2
Steel ships	no.	6,800.00	3,637.20	3,162.80	46.5
Tile	s/f	1.96	1.12	0.84	42.8
Fishnets	lbs.	2.00	1.20	0.80	40.0
Petroleum products	k/l	25.67	16.38	9.29	36.2
Sugar	m/t	110.00	86.83	23.17	21.0

[a]m/t = metric ton; c/s = case; s/f = square foot; k/l = kilo liter.

[b]Based on import price of import substitutes.

[c]Chemical textile yarn.

[d]The value of imported raw materials per unit price of import substitutes.

Source: The Analysis on Substitute Effect of Import Substitute Industry (Korea Productivity Center, 1965), p. 29.

141

about gradual private and social benefits in the long
run.

TABLE 4.5

Effect of Hypothetical Import-Substitution Project
(in millions of U.S. dollars)

Import-substitution production Direct savings in imports	15 per year
Imported capital equipment Initial year	20 nonrecurrent
Imported raw materials	4 per year
Imported complementary goods	2 per year

Effect on first year's
    balance of payments
	15 - (20 + 4 + 2)
	    = -11

Subsequent 9 years' balance of payments	135 - 54 = 81
Cumulative 10 year balance	-11 + 81 = 70

Note: This example, of course, assumes that there is
        no decline in exports in the course of import
        substitution. If, on the other hand, part of
        the import-substitute production is exported,
        the additional net-exchange saving should be
        taken into consideration.

Source: Peggy Musgrave, Trade Targets and Policies
         in Korea's Economic Development (Seoul:
         Economic Planning Board, 1965), p. 6. The
         illustration in this table is based mainly
         on Musgrave's work.

Effectiveness of Import Substitution

The effects of import substitution on the economy are complex. A better way of estimating them is
to see how much total output has increased as a result of import substitution. The values added of import substitutes show these effects. There is a risk
that the domestic factors allocated into import-
substitute industry might prove to have a negative-
value added. This means that the total cost of intermediate inputs would exceed the final value of the
output and implies that factors are allocated into
activities where their productivity is so low that
imported inputs are wasted.[16]

There are three basic values added to see the
effect of import substitutions: (1) domestic-value
added (Z_i) in industry i, (2) actual value added
(V_i), and (3) real-value added (W_i). The domestic-
value added has the normal meaning of value added,
which subtracts total inputs from gross value of output. Z_i can be expressed as $Z_i = X_i - (I_c + I_s)$,
where X_i denotes gross value of output i in domestic
prices, I_c denotes commodity inputs, and I_s denotes
service inputs.

The actual value added (V_i), in attempting to
get closer to the total effect of import substitution
on total output, adds nontraded-service inputs to
domestic-value added and subtracts only internation-
ally traded commodity inputs. V_i can be also expressed as $V_i = Z_i + I_s$.

Finally, the real value added (W_i) is value added in the absence of tariffs and subsidies on domestic
goods. The calculation of W_i without trade barriers
is possible by converting outputs and inputs at world
prices to domestic prices at the official exchange
rate.[17] The real-value added also includes nontraded-
service inputs, I_s. Again, W_i can be expressed in
equation form, namely:

$$W_i = \frac{X_i}{(1 + t_i)} + (B_i - S_i) - \frac{X_{ij}}{(1 + t_j)} + I_s$$

where X_{ij} = total deliveries from industry j
                  to industry i measured in domestic
                  prices

        B_i = total indirect taxes

        S_i = total subsidies such as tax exemp-
                tions and interest received by
                industry i

        t_i = nominal-tariff rate on domestic
               output

        t_j = nominal-tariff rate on input from
               industry j

    The values added are expressed as a percentage
of gross value of output (i) in domestic prices in
Table 4.6. As expected, all three kinds of value-
added rates are low, but they are not negative. But
the rate for actual-value added (V_i) is higher than
domestic-value added (X_i). The rate for real-value
added (W_i), excluding the net tariff and nontariff
subsidies, is usually the lowest among the three
values added. In the commodity-group comparisons,
the difference in the rates between W_i and V_i or Z_i
is wider in consumer goods than other goods. Furthermore, the value-added rates are generally low in consumer goods and intermediate products II (Table 4.6),
which require large percentages of both domestic and
foreign inputs and higher stages of production process.

    In conclusion, the amount of value added in the
import-substituting industry is higher as a result of
the whole complex of taxes, tariffs, and subsidies.
In order to achieve the assumed value of import substitution, the government is advised to encourage the
import-substitutes industry with high values added
to encourage the linkages forward and backward to
other industries.

Effectiveness of Protective Tariffs

    Usually, import substitution accompanies protec-
tive tariffs for the inefficient import-substitute

TABLE 4.6

Values-Added Rates of Selected Import Substitutes
(in percentages)

Commodity	Domestic Value Added z_i	Actual Value Added v_i	Real Value Added w_i
Intermediate Products I[a]			
Artificial resins	62.80	85.43	65.23
Hardboard	48.72	65.14	37.52
Paperboard	35.96	48.48	22.97
Tile	62.16	79.26	36.55
Average	52.41	69.58	40.58
Intermediate Products II[b]			
Iron and steel	13.48	19.93	17.23
Iron rods	12.15	19.89	17.45
Bolts	39.14	58.99	37.96
Pipe	27.61	29.16	9.61
Pistons	16.20	23.87	12.60
Average	21.72	30.37	18.93
Investment Goods			
Diesel engines	23.16	31.93	23.41
Diesel engines (agriculture)	34.30	43.93	25.13
Lathes	46.08	53.10	51.53
Electric capacitors	29.11	34.72	17.83
Average	33.16	40.92	29.43
Consumer Goods			
Meat products	12.44	18.69	5.89
Powdered milk	27.00	30.16	20.22
Margarine	18.99	27.30	31.02
Woolen fabric	45.72	67.79	30.02
Synthetic fabric	40.59	52.84	22.75
Average	28.95	47.96	21.98

[a]Intermediate products I are goods of which main inputs are unprocessed raw materials; [b]intermediate products II are goods at higher levels of fabrication.

Source: Industrial Profile of Korea (Economic Planning Board, 1966).

industry in the early period of industrialization.[18]
Some economists advocate tariffs in order to attract
labor from the present idle capacity or from the traditional sector of the economy to the import-
substitute industry. Higher rates of return on labor
and capital through tariffs are considered to be a
strong incentive in an economy such as Korea, where
wages in import-substitute manufacturing are higher
than in agriculture.[19]

In analyzing the effect of tariffs on the import-
substitute industry, the effective-tariff rate is
more appropriate than the nominal tariff rate. The
nominal-tariff rate in the tariff schedule might have
a restrictive-consumption effect on imports. But to
measure the resource-allocation effect of a tariff
structure, one must compute the protective rate for
each import-substitute production process--that is,
the effective-tariff rate. In other words, nominal
tariffs apply to commodities, but resources move as
between economic activities.[20] The effective-tariff
rate measures the protective rate for each activity.

The effective-tariff rate is the percentage increase in value added of an industry as a result of
the tariffs on imports competitive with outputs and
the tariffs on inputs. It thus depends not only on
the nominal tariffs of the commodity produced by the
import-substitute industry but also on the nominal
tariffs on imported inputs.[21] The tariffs on competing imports of an industry allow the domestic producer
to raise the price of his import-substitute product,
and in this respect, the tariff is a subsidy to import substitutes. On the other hand, the tariffs on
competing-intermediate and raw-materials inputs going
into import substitutes allow the domestic supplier
of such products to raise their prices, and in this
sense, the tariff is a tax on import substitutes.[22]

In order to compute the effective rate, not only
the tariffs but also other subsidies such as tax and
interest benefits are taken into account in Table
4.7.[23] There are two kinds of effective-protective
rates--one implicit-subsidy rate on value added in
the absence of protection (E_1) and the other on value

added with protection (E_2). In calculating the effective rates, the numerator $(V_i - W_i)$ is nothing but
the net subsidy.

The effective-tariff rates (E_1) in Korea are in
all cases higher than the nominal rates on the import-
substitute output. It may be safe to say that industrialization has been pursued behind a wall of protective tariffs which have provided generous incentives
for the establishment in Korea of import-substituting
industries. To put the argument differently, the
higher the effective-protection rate, the more likely
is the domestic industry to become an effective-
import substitute.

In the commodity-group comparisons, of protective
rates, both E_1 and E_2 in consumer goods are substantially higher than any other group. The next important group is intermediate products I (Table 4.7).
The least-protected industries are those producing
heavy machinery and transport equipment.[24] The greater emphasis on the protection of consumer goods and
intermediate products I is understandable because the
markets existing in Korea are primarily for consumer
goods and light manufactured goods. Consumer goods
by and large, require less capital investment than
other industries and often less skilled manpower, two
factors which tend to be scarce in the Korean economy.
But, for long-run planning, the encouragement of investment industries should not be neglected.

Persistent overvaluation of the Korean won should
be taken into account when evaluating the effective-
protection rates shown in Table 4.7. All other studies
on effective-tariff rates, as cited previously, assume
an exchange rate that reflects the scarcity price of
foreign exchange. This assumption means that the domestic price of any import substitute is equal to the
world price of a competing import plus domestic taxes
on imports. This assumption is invalid in the case
of Korea. The overvalued exchange rate understates
the protection actually afforded by the tariff rates
shown in Table 4.7. As mentioned before, Korean currency has over the years been consistently overvalued
by various degrees.

TABLE 4.7

Nominal- and Effective-Tariff Rates in Korea, 1965
(in percentages)

Commodity	Nominal Rate on Output[a]	Nominal Rate on Input[a]	Effective Tariff Rates[b] $E_1 = \dfrac{V_i - W_i}{W_i}$ [c]	Effective Tariff Rates[b] $E_2 = \dfrac{V_i - W_i}{V_i}$ [d]
Intermediate Products I[e]				
Inorganic chemicals	20.95	20.85	20.59	16.81
Other inorganic chemicals	29.31	28.80	28.53	22.03
Artificial resins	31.86	16.58	47.11	32.02
Leather	60.07	26.19	126.16	55.78
Cork products	35.00	15.25	50.08	33.37
Paper products	37.29	9.98	17.22	47.25
Cement	15.00	29.16	8.74	8.35
Stone goods	50.00	12.28	135.64	55.19
Refractory bricks	46.67	15.43	84.00	43.83
Asbestos	50.94	14.31	59.59	37.34
Glass wares	80.00	11.44	106.19	51.50
Silica	14.64	16.16	13.94	12.30
Average	39.3	17.9	64.8	34.6
Intermediate Products II[f]				
Petroleum products	25.8	1.38	103.46	50.60
Printing ink	60.00	31.34	67.57	40.32
Chemical fertilizers	10.88	12.81	2.56	1.93
Insecticides	15.90	17.71	14.29	12.50
Chemical fibers	56.79	26.78	128.56	55.15

Commodity	Nominal Rate on Output[a]	Nominal Rate on Input[a]	Effective Tariff Rates[b] $E_1 = \dfrac{V_i - W_i}{W_i}$ [c]	$E_2 = \dfrac{V_i - W_i}{V_i}$ [d]
Nylon fishnet	35.00	23.16	48.07	32.47
Iron ingots	16.39	10.79	20.10	16.45
Iron rods	20.78	8.90	50.05	32.72
Steel bars	23.36	16.36	32.10	23.29
Copper	30.00	10.19	73.47	42.35
Metal products	45.92	11.92	104.73	49.82
Measuring instruments	45.75	18.34	82.84	44.91
Average	32.1	15.8	60.7	33.5
Investment Goods				
Boilers (industrial)	59.41	15.01	146.88	59.29
Lathes	12.90	12.38	18.93	14.29
Industrial machines	30.99	14.98	52.20	31.49
Locomotives	21.11	20.66	18.85	15.86
Rectifiers	34.84	22.63	56.42	35.48
Electric wire	36.69	19.23	89.36	45.50
Communication equipment	45.57	25.46	66.03	34.42
Other electric equipment	48.74	26.22	81.45	44.71
Steel ships	28.88	19.63	40.21	28.68
Average	35.5	19.6	63.4	34.4

(Continued)

149

TABLE 4.7 - Continued

Commodity	Nominal Rate on Output[a]	Nominal Rate on Input[a]	Effective Tariff Rates[b]	
			$E1 = \dfrac{V_i - W_i}{W_i}$ [c]	$E2 = \dfrac{V_i - W_i}{V_i}$ [d]
Consumer Goods				
Wheat flour	53.40	19.16	111.73	52.77
Sugar	39.83	25.38	45.77	31.39
Vegetable oil	31.93	20.20	48.20	32.46
Caustic soda	58.48	33.24	93.13	48.22
Antibiotics	23.82	22.54	24.27	19.53
Paper products	80.00	50.50	131.01	56.71
(Synthetic) yarn	100.00	36.47	226.65	69.39
Soap	87.18	23.59	184.17	64.81
Glass products	80.00	25.41	136.30	57.68
Household hardware	64.57	21.40	218.79	65.57
Electric appliances	65.69	17.01	208.98	67.64
Steam boilers	70.00	13.55	241.10	70.68
Average	62.9	25.7	139.2	53.1

aNominal rates are weighted averages of tariffs on output and imported inputs of import substitutes on cost, insurance, and freight prices.

bTax and interest incentives in calculating effective tariff rates are negligible.

cThe E_1 type of effective rate is employed by Johnson, Balassa, and Corden. (See Bibliography.)

dThe E_2 type of effective rate is used by Soligo and Stern.

eIntermediate products I are goods of which main inputs are unprocessed raw materials.

fIntermediate products II are goods at higher levels of fabrication.

Source: A Report on Import Substitute Industry in Korea (Seoul National University, 1967), pp. 134-47.

IMPORT LIBERALIZATION

The volume of imports in Korea has been affected by changes in import policies. The general trend
of import policy has been toward liberalization of
<u>quantitative</u> trade and exchange restrictions. In the
past, the major tool of protective policy had been
direct prohibition of imports and quota restrictions.
Recently, however, the emphasis has shifted to indirect protection through tariffs. Both direct and
indirect protections have helped promote import-
substitute industries, but indirect restrictions on
the basis of incentives are the economically sound
policy.

As a part of liberalization programs, Korea
joined the IMF in 1955 and GATT in 1966. Korea
agreed, as a prerequisite of membership in these organizations, to eliminate trade restrictions gradually as its balance of payments improves. Korea has
not yet accepted Article VIII of IMF or Article XI
of GATT, but that acceptance may be near.[25]

Article VIII of the IMF Agreement and Article
XI of the GATT Agreement make provisions for general
elimination of quantitative restrictions. Article
VIII of the IMF Agreement reads:

> Subject to provisions of Article VII,
> Section 3(b) and Article XIV, Section 2,
> no member shall, without the approval
> of the Fund, impose restrictions on the
> making of payments and transfer for cur-
> rent international transactions.[26]

Article XI of GATT makes a similar provision:

> No prohibition or restrictions other than
> duties, taxes, or other charges, whether
> made effective through import quotas, im-
> port or export licenses or other measures,
> shall be instituted or maintained by a
> contracting party on the importation of
> any product . . .[27]

The first installment of import liberalization was effected in May, 1964, at the time of the exchange reform that established a fluctuating-exchange rate. Before 1964, Korea maintained quarterly import quotas by commodity in accordance with complicated regulations and decrees,[28] and the country had enormous trade deficits. In recent years, as industrial production and exports expanded, it became reasonable to attempt trade liberalization.

The general philosophy of import policy has changed from quantitative restrictions on imports to measures to increase the cost of imports. Import quotas by commodity have been abolished while tariffs and margin requirements on import loans have been raised, and the share of import financing based on D/P (document against payment), D/A (document against acceptance), or banker's usance, has been reduced. D/P, D/A, and banker's usance are all import-financing methods without letters of credit, and all imply larger credit use than would be possible by means of letters of credit.

There are two basic measurements of import liberalization. One way of measuring the degree of import liberalization is to compare the number of goods that can be imported without direct restrictions with the total number of imported goods. Another measure is to compare the amount of imports automatically approved with the total value of imports. Data for this measurement are not available in Korea.

As shown in Table 4.8, the number of goods free of direct restrictions increased from none in the automatic-approval list (AA) in the first half of 1964 to 3,761 in June, 1967. The number of restricted items, on the other hand, decreased from 1,124 in the first half of 1964 to zero in June, 1967. The share of AA's increased from 8 percent in the second half of 1964 to 97.6 percent of total-import items in June, 1967. At first, the AA list covered mainly capital goods and raw materials while semirestricted (SR) and restricted (R) items were mainly manufactured-consumer goods. A majority of prohibited items (P) consisted of so-called nonessentials and luxuries.[29]

TABLE 4.8

Import Liberalization by Number of Commodities
(in number)

Classifi-cation	January-June 1964 No.	%	July-December 1964 No.	%	December 1, 1965 No.	%	June 1, 1966 No.	%	December 1, 1966 No.	%	June 1, 1967 No.	%
AA[a]	–	0	31	8.0	1,648	92.7	2,236	94.7	2,946	94.8	3,761	97.6
SR[b]	–	0	37	9.5	118	6.6	114	4.8	163	5.2	91	2.4
R[c]	1,124	100	320	82.5	12	0.7	12	0.5	–	–	–	–
Total	1,124	100.0	388	100.0	1,778	100.0	2,362	100.0	3,109	100.0	3,852	100.0
P[d]	617	–	629	–	589	–	387	–	362	–	244	–

Note (–) indicates none.
[a] AA is automatic-approval time.
[b] SR is semirestricted item.
[c] R is restricted item.
[d] P is prohibited item.

Source: Monthly Statistical Review (Bank of Korea, July, 1964), p. 54; (September, 1966),
p. 12; (June, 1967), p. 54.

153

The import-liberalization program was highlight-
ed by the establishment of the "negative-list" system
in July, 1967.[30] The system was changed from a
"positive-list" to a "negative-list" approach, which
meant that henceforth all imports would be automatically approved unless specifically listed on the
negative list. Previously, only items eligible for
import either automatically or by restriction were
listed, leaving a wide range of "unlisted" items in-
eligible for importation.

The present system does not imply a complete
elimination of quantitative restrictions. As of
January, 1968, there were about 320 items which were
restricted and 135 items subject to quotas.[31] Although individual import quotas on most items were
eliminated, there was still an over-all limit on imports in accordance with the government-trade program
and foreign-exchange budget. On top of protective
tariffs, the Korean Ministry of Commerce and Industry
exercises a considerable although indirect influence
over imports through its system of registering quali-
fied importers and through its many informal contacts
with business enterprises.

To what extent the increase in imports is the
effect of the official trade-liberalization policy is
not easy to assess. But the Korean Government has
at times threatened to reinstitute quantitative restrictions, arguing that the increase in imports in
recent years was directly caused by import liberalization.

Such a backward step would be unsound because
most nonessential consumer goods remain restrained
by quotas or tariffs. The tariff rate on many luxury
goods such as cosmetics, watches, and automobiles is
over 100 percent. Furthermore, most of the import
increases of recent years has not been in consumer
goods but in machinery and raw materials, which are
of vital importance to import substitution and industrialization. Finally, foreign competition is healthy
in combating inefficiency and monopolistic power among
domestic producers and in taking advantage of foreign
technology and innovations.

In summary, the import-GNP ratio in Korea has increased in recent years, partly because the import of capital goods and raw materials is required for the initial development of import-substitute industries and partly because the increase in income could afford the import of foreign goods after the relaxation of quantitative restrictions. But there are many reasons to believe, as discussed in this chapter, that the demand for imported capital and consumer goods will decline as industrialization proceeds with import substitution in the long run.

Furthermore, the import-substitute industry can be more effectively protected if a realistic exchange rate is established and if the cost of import financing is raised. Because the Korean won is overvalued, the import of foreign goods is still profitable in some cases. In short, the decrease of the import-GNP ratio from 20 percent during the first five years of our projection (1967-71) to 19 percent during the following five years (1972-76) does not seem unattainable.

NOTES

1. S. S. Kanesa-Thasan, "Stabilizing an Economy --The Korean Experience," a paper presented at the Conference on Korean Planning, Northwestern University, June 19-21, 1968, p. 19. (Mimeographed.)

2. IBRD mission to Korea in 1968.

3. Monthly Statistical Review (Seoul: Bank of Korea, April, 1963), p. 5.

4. Economic Survey (Seoul: Economic Planning Board, 1967), pp. 129-30.

5. "Import Substitution and Export Diversification," Economic Survey of Asia and the Far East (United Nations Commission for Asia and the Far East, 1963), pp. 5-112.

6. See Staffan Burenstam Linder, Trade and Trade Policy for Development (New York: Frederick A. Praeger, 1967), p. 89.

7. Albert D. Hirschman, The Strategy of Economic Development (New Haven: Yale University Press, 1958), p. 98.

8. "Import Substitution and Export Diversification," op. cit., pp. 5-17.

9. Ibid., pp. 28-29.

10. N. H. Leff and D. Netto, "Import Substitution, Foreign Investment, and International Disequilibrium," The Journal of Development Studies (April, 1966), pp. 219-23.

11. David B. Humphrey, "Note on Import Substitution: The Case of Brazil," The Journal of Development Studies (October, 1966), pp. 70-75.

12. Hirschman, op. cit., p. 212.

13. See Humphrey, op. cit., p. 77; also see C. F. Diaz-Alexandro, "On the Import Intensity of Import Substitution," Kyklos, Vol. XVIII (1965), Fasc. 3, pp. 495-509.

14. Linder, op. cit., p. 92.

15. Diaz-Alexandro, op. cit.

16. Linder, op. cit., pp. 84-85.

17. See R. Soligo and J. Stern, "Tariff Protection, Import Substitution and Industrial Efficiency," Pakistan Development Review (Summer, 1965), pp. 249-69; A Report on Import Substitute Industry in Korea (Seoul: Seoul National University, 1967), pp. 9-10; Harry Johnson, Economic Policies Toward Less Developed Countries (Washington, D.C.: The Brookings Institution, 1967), pp. 170-73.

18. For instance, see Johnson, op. cit., pp. 71-73; Soligo and Stern, op. cit., pp. 249-69; and Hal Lary, Imports of Manufactures from Less Developed Countries (New York: National Bureau of Economic Research, 1968), pp. 10-11.

19. E. E. Hagen, "An Economic Justification of Protectionism," Quarterly Journal of Economics (November, 1958), pp. 496-514.

20. W. H. Corden, "The Structure of a Tariff System and the Effective Protective Rate," Journal of Political Economy (June, 1966), p. 222.

21. Ibid.

22. See H. G. Grubel and H. G. Johnson, "Nominal Tariffs, Indirect Taxes and Effective Rates of Protection, the Common Market Countries 1959," Economic Journal (December, 1967), pp. 761-76.

23. A Report on Import Substitute Industry, op. cit., p. 39.

24. Ibid., pp. 10-32.

25. The Korean Trade Structure and Policies (Seoul: Ministry of Finance, 1967), pp. 50-51.

26. Articles of Agreement (Washington, D.C.: International Monetary Fund, 1944), p. 15.

27. Final Act of GATT (United Nations, 1947), pp. 22-23.

28. Review of Korean Economy, 1964 (Seoul: Bank of Korea, 1965), p. 101.

29. Monthly Statistical Review, op. cit. (January, 1967), p. 89.

30. Ibid. (August, 1967), p. 64.

31. Correspondence with the Korean Ministry of Commerce and Industry; also Allocation of Foreign Exchanges for Imports (Seoul: Ministry of Commerce and Industry, 1968).

CHAPTER **5** DOMESTIC FINANCING FOR
INVESTMENT REQUIREMENTS

INTRODUCTION

In Chapter 2, external-capital needs were estimated in terms of the internal gap as well as in
terms of the external gap; the latter was larger and
hence dominant for most of the projection period. In
the past, the bulk of investment requirements has
been financed by foreign savings, but the share of
domestic savings has increased substantially in recent years. In order to achieve the relatively high
marginal-savings rate during our projection period
and to achieve a self-sustaining economy without foreign aid, domestic savings must bear the major burden
of financing investment requirements. Domestic capital can be mobilized by employing financial and fiscal techniques.

INVESTMENT STRATEGY FOR DEVELOPMENT

Investment strategy has been influenced by the
various economic programs and plans formulated and
executed by changing governments. These economic
programs can be discussed under four headings, namely,
(1) the Nathan Report, (2) abortive plans, (3) the
First Five-Year Economic Plan, and (4) the Second
Five-Year Economic Plan.

The Nathan Report

The first attempt at comprehensive economic plan-
ning in Korea was a study done for the U.N. Korean
Reconstruction Agency (UNKRA) by a U.S. firm which
Robert Nathan headed. The report, which dealt with

the postwar reconstruction of the Korean economy,
was published in 1954 as a broad five-year economic
plan.[1]

The report initiated aggregate planning projections in Korea. It derived rather arbitrary aggregate targets and resource requirements, such as those
for investment, and it tried to translate these ag-
gregates into industrial details. Planned investment
in industry was geared mainly to meeting the estimated
demands from other sectors. Programs were checked
for internal consistency and trimmed to fit within
the prospectively available resources.[2] The Nathan
Report repeatedly emphasized the need for internal
and over-all consistency, and various investment programs were appropriately balanced in terms of supply
and demand. But it is not clear how these balances
were achieved.[3]

Although the Nathan Plan was never adopted by
the Korean Government, it was at least technically
adequate and established standards of unbiased economic analysis for future Korean planners. Furthermore, it provided guidelines for future planning. But
Korea had no operative planning until 1958.

Abortive Plans

The lack of comprehensive planning may have contributed to the mismanagement of economic resources
in a shortage-plagued economy.[4] Setbacks in economic
growth were partially caused by the lack of balanced-
investment planning. Certain industries expanded beyond existing demand while others fell behind. Thus,
electric power was not able to keep up with growing
requirements while textiles and cement produced surpluses.

To remedy these imbalances, the government began
late in 1958 to develop economic planning by estab-
lishing the Economic Development Council within the
Ministry of Reconstruction. In the spring of 1959,
the council submitted a three-year plan to the Cabinet. The macroeconomic framework used in formulating
the plan was a "Colm-type" model which stressed

employment objectives and based investment requirements on specified capital-labor ratios in a number
of sectors.[5] Thus, the over-all output projections
were derived from assumed employment and labor-
productivity targets. There were no clear criteria
for selecting investment projects, and consequently,
decisions on the investment program were based mainly
on the judgment of consulting committees. In the
spring of 1960, the Cabinet approved the three-year
plan, but shortly after its approval, the Rhee Regime
was ousted, and the plan was set aside.

By the end of 1960, the new regime under the
leadership of Prime Minister Chang Myun instructed
the Economic Development Council to draw up a new
five-year development plan that would supersede the
earlier plan. In contrast to the "balanced-growth"
pattern of the three-year plan, the new plan stressed
the need for concentrating investment in a few "leading sectors," particularly power, coal, cement, and
social-overhead capital. Whereas the three-year plan
had proceeded from a labor-oriented model, as noted,
the five-year plan was based on a capital-oriented
Harrod-Domar model focusing on capital-output ratios
for the key sectors of the economy as the main parameters.[6]

The stress in the new plan was on heavy public
investment and industrialization. The draft was completed just prior to the military coup of May, 1961,
and it was not acceptable to the new government. But
the 1961 plan provided a basis for a third planning
attempt which was finally carried through to comple-
tion as the First Five-Year Economic Plan (1962-66).

The First Five-Year Economic Plan

The Economic Planning Board replaced the Economic Development Council in July, 1961, and it assumed
the over-all responsibility to draw up the first plan.
The strategy underlying the first plan was to place
emphasis on three "key" or "leading" sectors, namely,
electric power, manufacturing, and social-overhead
capital.[7] Consequently, of the total investment of
$2,473 million during the plan period, approximately

48.8 percent was to be allocated for power, transportation, and communication; another 34 percent to manufacturing; and only 17 percent to agriculture.[8]
Investments in commerce and industries were to be
minimized.

The Harrod-Domar investment model continued to
be used to estimate the aggregate amount of investment requirements, but it was modified to allow for
different growth targets in primary, secondary, and
tertiary industries. The aggregate estimate was
checked against microeconomic estimates of investments, using sectoral, incremental, capital-output
ratios. The sectoral estimates were rough and not
reliable because detailed data on sectoral capital-
output ratios and interindustry input-output schedules
were not available at the time. Thus, there was no
good basis for checking the consistency of the estimate in macro- and microterms; allocation took place
in accordance with the key-sector objectives.

The emphasis on investment in a few key industries in the plan was reflected in the actual composition of investment, including both public and private investments. The ratio of fixed investment to
total investment in the mining and manufacturing sector rose to 32.6 percent in 1966 from 22.4 percent in
1957-61; social overhead increased slightly to 31.6
percent in 1962-66 from 30.1 percent in 1957-61 (see
Table 5.1). On the other hand, the investment ratio
in agriculture and other service sectors declined.
Since the absolute amount of investment in all sectors increased in 1962-66 compared with the 1957-61
level, the change in the structure of investment was
not accompanied by sacrifices of other sectors but
was accompanied by emphasis in the relative composition of investment in key industries.

The structural change in Korean investments has
been possible because the government has enough means
to influence the private sector to invest funds in
accordance with planning. Most financial institutions
are owned by the government, tax and interest benefits
are given to priority industries, and permission and
preferential tariffs are given to the import of

TABLE 5.1

Industrial Components of Gross Domestic Fixed-Capital Formation
(in billions of won)

	Current Prices 1957–61	1962	1963	1964	1965	1966	1962–66
Agriculture, forestry, and fisheries	16.44 (13.0)	4.03 (8.3)	7.01 (10.3)	9.65 (12.0)	13.67 (11.6)	24.83 (12.4)	59.19 (11.4)
Mining and manufacturing	28.35 (22.4)	10.39 (21.4)	16.04 (23.6)	20.1 (24.8)	31.95 (27.2)	67.05 (32.5)	145.44 (27.9)
Mining and quarrying	1.62 (1.3)	0.38 (0.8)	0.87 (1.3)	0.78 (0.9)	1.49 (1.3)	2.11 (1.0)	5.63 (1.1)
Manufacturing	26.73 (21.1)	10.01 (20.6)	15.17 (22.3)	19.23 (23.9)	30.46 (25.9)	64.94 (31.5)	139.81 (26.8)
Social overhead capital	38.11 (30.1)	18.26 (37.5)	26.31 (38.6)	24.33 (30.2)	32.60 (27.7)	63.38 (30.8)	164.88 (31.6)
Electricity, water, and sanitary services	6.86 (5.4)	5.22 (10.7)	8.63 (10.7)	6.36 (7.9)	7.10 (6.0)	10.48 (5.1)	37.79 (7.2)
Transportation, storage, and communication	29.95 (23.7)	11.45 (23.5)	16.28 (23.9)	16.93 (21.0)	24.06 (20.5)	50.80 (24.7)	119.52 (22.9)
Construction	1.30 (1.0)	1.59 (3.3)	1.40 (2.0)	1.04 (1.3)	1.44 (1.2)	2.10 (1.0)	7.57 (1.5)
Housing and other services	43.75 (34.5)	15.94 (32.8)	18.68 (27.5)	26.55 (33.0)	39.42 (33.5)	50.73 (24.6)	151.32 (29.1)
Housing	19.69 (15.5)	5.81 (11.9)	6.91 (10.2)	10.48 (13.0)	13.92 (11.8)	21.18 (9.8)	58.30 (11.2)
Wholesale and retail trade	6.26 (4.9)	2.76 (5.7)	3.20 (4.7)	3.95 (4.9)	7.84 (6.7)	7.81 (3.8)	25.56 (4.9)
Banking, insurance, and real estate	0.53 (0.5)	0.13 (0.3)	0.13 (0.2)	0.28 (0.4)	0.50 (0.4)	0.98 (0.5)	2.02 (0.5)
Public administration and defense	4.31 (3.4)	0.92 (1.9)	1.39 (2.0)	1.21 (1.5)	1.96 (1.7)	2.48 (1.2)	7.96 (1.5)
Services	12.96 (10.2)	6.32 (13.0)	7.05 (10.4)	10.63 (13.2)	15.20 (12.9)	18.28 (8.9)	57.48 (11.0)
Total	(100.0)	(100.0)	(100.0)	(100.0)	(100.0)	(100.0)	(100.0)

Note: ( ) Figures in parentheses denote percentages of the total.
Source: Economic Statistics Yearbook (The Bank of Korea, 1967).

industrial goods which are required for investment
plans. The Korean plan is somewhat similar to the
French indicative plan.[9]

The Second Five-Year Economic Plan

The second plan was a continuation of the first
plan and a part of long-range goals which extend to
1981. But the second plan was better organized to
combine an adequate technical base and the involve-
ment of domestic as well as foreign interest groups
(including the Nathan Mission, the German consultation group, academics, and Korea's economic minis-
tries), in the preparation and review of the plan.[10]
Also, patterns and procedures had been developed for
translating planning guidelines into policy actions
and for revising the plan targets to respond to
changing circumstances.

The ratio of investment allocations by industrial groups in the second plan is about the same as
in the first plan, but the emphasis has been shifted
to export- and import- substitute industries. Continuous development of infrastructure sectors is
scheduled. However, unlike the first plan, the investment program in the second plan is the result of
three coordinated programs.[11] First, an aggregate
or macroapproach sets out the preliminary estimate
for the plan period of total investment requirements.
Second, at the level of maximum possible disaggrega-
tion, the development of a detailed project program
is made to determine specific investments necessary
for carrying out the plan. Finally, a sectoral-
projection model bridges the gap between these two
extremes, primarily by translating the macroforecast
into demand for individual projects.[12]

According to traditional investment criteria, an
investment project is carried out if the rate of return on investment is greater than the cost of capital or if the value of the investment discounted to
the present is greater than the total cost of the investment. In the case of Korea, an internal rate of
return was used in evaluating agricultural-investment
projects.[13] This method does not seem to be

reasonable, because there is no adequate-earnings or cost information on land reclamation and irrigation projects. Furthermore, the selection of an appropriate discount rate is difficult because the cost of capital is not readily definable. The true cost of foreign capital is often higher than the foreign price translated into won because of the overvalued exchange rate; and the interest cost on bank loans varies depending upon the type of investment projects, although these differentials may, of course, in part reflect genuine risk differences.

The investment criteria used in manufacturing and social-overhead capital are not directly related to any cost-benefit analysis but rather to the government's planning for industrialization and social objectives.[14] Other supplementary criteria are measures of the project's employment-creation effects and foreign-exchange earnings potential.

In order to avoid bottlenecks or surpluses, investment decisions are coordinated among interrelated industries. The existing input-output table was updated in 1965 to improve the sectoral-model demand projections, from which investment requirements by industry are in turn derived. But there remains an inherent problem--failure to take into account factors such as the differential growth of markets and changing, interindustry coefficients such as are induced by newly emerging economies of scale.

Investment strategies have thus been mainly influenced by economic plans that have in turn been subject to the existing political environment. The Nathan Plan received a chilly reception because of poor political relations between President Rhee and Nathan Associates.[15] As a result of the ouster of the Rhee Regime, his three-year plan was replaced by a new plan, as stated earlier. This 1961 plan was superceded by the 1962 plan as a result of a military coup. It is understandable that in a country such as Korea the government plays a major role in investment programs. The government owns most financial institutions and approves foreign-capital imports tailored to pursue planning objectives. But this political

influence on investment decisions has economic costs.
Whether they are derived from a "balanced" or from
an "unbalanced" growth model, investment decisions
must at a minimum have internal consistency regard-
less of political changes to achieve longer-term economic aims. In fact, the controversy involving balanced vs. unbalanced growth may be an empty debate.
Balanced growth is impossible without a few leading
industries, while unbalanced growth will in the long
run lead to balanced growth.[16]

FINANCIAL TECHNIQUES AND THE MOBILIZATION
OF SAVINGS

In all countries, financial techniques bear im-
portantly on the ability to mobilize savings. What
is needed is a transformation of the financial system.[17] In a traditional economy, investment funds
are generated internally--from retained earnings and
depreciation. The function of financial intermediaries involves the transmission of savings from savers to investors through creation of liabilities to
savers and purchasing of debt securities of investors. Hidden savings can be attracted through offer-
ing new types of financial assets to savers, and these
funds are most efficiently allocated through financial institutions. The flow of savings through financial channels is governed by a complex of interest
rates in either explicit or implicit form and by some
direct controls.[18]

Price Stability

A degree of price stability is a prerequisite of
the smooth operation of financial techniques, and
thus of the mobilization of domestic savings.[19] Inflation taxes most fixed-return financial assets and
penalizes savers who have foregone consumption. Their
inevitable response is to withhold savings from those
channels and to divert them either to consumption, to
"inflation-proof" assets, or to inefficient forms of
investment through unorganized financial markets.
There is evidence of considerable skepticism regarding price stabilization on the part of Korean savers.

Relatively low demand for money and savings deposits even during intervals of price stability implies that savers expect instability.[20] If this is so, it may take some time to remove their suspicions. Price stability has to last for some time.

Inflation has been a serious and chronic disease of the Korean economy, although improvement has occurred in recent years. During the Korean War and the reconstruction period, inflation was massive. Between 1953 and 1956, the wholesale-price index doubled. Even the large inflow of foreign aid could not cope with the pressing demands of social and economic reconstruction, and the government continuously resorted to deficit financing through monetary expansion.

The first financial-stabilization program was formulated on April 15, 1957, by the Combined Economic Board (CEB). (CEB itself was established under the Agreement of Economic Coordination between the Republic of Korea and the U.N. Command in May, 1952, and is the administrative instrumentality entrusted with the task of coordinating U.S.-Korean economic policies.) The main thrust of this fifteen-point program was to maintain price stability by controlling the money supply. Budgetary expenditures were to be limited to the amount of tax receipts, the volume of new credit to that of savings, and investment of counterpart funds of aid to collections of counterpart funds.[21] This program was continued in 1958 and greatly contributed to reducing inflation. However, the program collapsed between 1961 and 1963 as the military regime engaged in an ill-conceived policy of monetary expansion. This situation was corrected in the latter years of the first plan, and annual price increases averaged 9 percent in 1965-66.

The Korean inflation can be analyzed in terms of changes in the money supply. The money supply of a country should not, in general, grow at a rate in excess of the rate of growth of real income from current production and foreign aid. Actually, it may grow at a rate somewhat in excess of this without provoking inflation, to the extent that the shrinkage

in the nonmonetary sector of the economy, the growth
of wealth, the growing differentiation of production,
and other such factors involve a growing demand from
the public for money at any given level of prices
(so that income velocity declines).[22]

If, however, the money supply grows faster than
at this noninflationary rate, the result can only be
inflationary pressures and general price rises. This
is exactly what has been happening in Korea. Table
5.2 shows that the average annual rate of growth in
Korea's real GNP in 1953-68 has been about 7 percent
per annum. But the money supply has been growing
at a rate of 31 percent per annum. The result has
been a continuing price rise, at a rate of 20 percent
per year, although that has admittedly of late declined.

One interesting point is that in some cases
prices vary at different rates before the money supply varies. This means that the cause of Korean inflation can also be analyzed in terms of the excessive
aggregate demand over the supply of goods and services
available to the economy.

As shown in Table 5.3, the increase in the money
supply was largely attributable, until 1956, to bank
borrowing of the public sector, which was considerably larger than that of the private sector. Since
1956, however, net bank credit to the public sector
has tended to decline as a result of increasing government deposits with the Bank of Korea. This was
possible through sales of foreign-aid goods at frequently devalued exchange rates, which sales in turn
withdrew currency from the public. This favorable
effect, however, has been more than offset since 1956
by bank credit to the private sector. Since 1965,
it should be noted, net bank credit to the private
sector has tended to go down as a result of the tight-
liquidity control which is part of the stabilization
program.

A new element in the monetary picture since 1966
has been the expansionary effect of the foreign sector. Net foreign-exchange receipts have risen rapidly

TABLE 5.2

Significant Economic Indicators

Year	Money Supply[a] Amount[b]	%[c]	Deflated Gross National Product Amount[d]	%[c]	Wholesale Price Index[e] Amount	%[c]
1953	3,032	–	421.93	–	26.5	–
1954	5,808	91.6	447.36	6.0	34.0	28.3
1955	9,352	61.0	474.54	6.1	61.5	80.9
1956	12,093	29.3	480.47	1.2	81.0	31.7
1957	14,518	20.1	522.73	8.8	94.1	16.6
1958	19,255	32.6	551.69	5.5	88.2	-6.3
1959	23,286	20.9	575.84	4.4	90.3	2.4
1960	24,509	5.2	589.07	2.3	100.0	10.7
1961	34,411	40.2	613.61	4.2	113.2	13.2
1962	40,816	18.6	634.97	3.5	123.8	9.4
1963	41,355	1.3	693.03	9.1	149.3	20.6
1964	48.580	17.4	750.31	8.3	201.1	34.7
1965	64,699	33.1	805.85	7.4	100.0	10.0
1966	84,179	30.1	913.82	13.4	108.8	8.8
1967	120,028	42.2	995.16	8.9	115.8	6.8
1968	149,840	24.8	1,127.32	13.2	125.2	8.1
Average		31.2		6.8		20.1

[a]The sum of currency in circulation, checking deposits, passbook deposits, public deposits, and all other monetary deposits with all banking institutions.
[b]In millions of won.
[c]All percentage figures are year-to-year percentage changes.
[d]In billions of won.
[e]The base year is 1960 for the years 1953-64 and 1965 for the years 1965-68.

Sources: Price Statistics Summary (The Bank of Korea, 1966); Economic Statistics Yearbook (The Bank of Korea, 1967); Monthly Economic Statistics (The Bank of Korea, November, 1969).

TABLE 5.3

Principal Sectors Affecting the Money Supply
(in millions of won)

Year	Money Supply	Bank Credit to Public Sector[a]	Bank Credit to Private Sector[b]	Foreign Sector[c]	Other
1953	3,032	1,697	1,362	88	-115
1954	5,808	4,018	1,842	14	-66
1955	9,352	7,498	3,075	-1,040	-181
1956	12,093	6,945	5,675	-35	-492
1957	14,518	5,856	9,249	472	-1,050
1958	19,255	3,622	14,012	1,988	-367
1959	23,286	5,316	15,123	2,255	592
1960	24,509	1,012	21,244	3,340	-1,087
1961	34,411	5,651	24,036	10,575	-5,851
1962	40,816	9,290	30,924	6,938	-6,336
1963	41,355	11,003	37,837	-6,661	-824
1964	48,580	7,521	41,316	-1,941	1,684
1965	64,699	15,698	43,293	6,437	-729
1966	84,179	12,160	33,187	41,540	-2,718
1967	120,028	11,541	43,059	78,088	-12,660
1968	149,840	7,326	51,163	105,861	-14,510

[a] Includes government overdrafts at the Bank of Korea minus government deposits with the Bank of Korea, government bonds held by all banking institutions, claims on local governments of banking institutions, loans to government agencies by the Bank of Korea, and government lending to all banking institutions.

[b] Includes loans by all banking institutions, stocks and debentures, time and savings deposits (negative factors).

[c] Includes net purchases of foreign exchange and deposits of foreign organizations (negative factors).

Sources: Economic Statistics Yearbook (Bank of Korea, 1967); Monthly Economic Statistics (Bank of Korea, November, 1969).

as the result of the expansion of exports, invisible
earnings and remittances from abroad, plus the fact
that increasing proportions of imports have been
covered by short- and long-term liabilities.[23]

The Korean Government has continued to be mainly responsible for the increase in the money supply
and for inflation, as will be explained shortly. It
is not the stabilization program itself that is at
fault, but rather the lack of a financial system to
carry it out. As mentioned before, all banking institutions are largely owned and controlled by the
government. Loan decisions are only to a limited
extent made by the financial institutions themselves.
The bulk of bank credit to the public sector consists
of government overdrafts at the Bank of Korea and
government bonds held by the banking institutions.

The Bank of Korea and other banking institutions
have no choice but to make available the funds necessary to finance a budgetary deficit. Even a large
part of bank credit to the private sector consists of
loans to government-owned corporations and to private
enterprises recommended by the government. The monetary expansion originating in the foreign sector
could have been "sterilized" more effectively by reducing credits to other sectors, especially the public sector. In short, the financial institutions
mainly act as instruments to allocate resources along
the lines of government preferences.

The Role of Financial Institutions

The financial system in Korea can be divided
into an official sector and an unofficial one. The
official sector consists of financial institutions.
The unofficial sector comprises the curb market with
individual money brokers and keh, which are rotating
credit cooperatives of wealthy ladies. Gurley and
his associates estimated the size of unofficial markets in the order of 40-45 billion won, representing
close to one quarter of private-sector financial assets.[24] Funds obtained through the unofficial sector
are frequently used for nonproductive investment such
as speculation in real estate, foreign exchange, and

other risky businesses. On the other hand, indirect
financing through financial institutions is advantageous, partly because the institutions pool savings
funds from thousands of individuals in unofficial
markets and are thus able to make large loans safely,
and partly because the institutions are managed by
professionals who are able to investigate and analyze
potential borrowers carefully and allocate loan funds
to the most productive users.

The Bank of Korea (which is the central bank)
and commercial banks are the traditional financial
institutions. The assets of the Bank of Korea consist mainly of foreign exchange and loans to the
government, while its liabilities are mainly the currency issue and deposits of government and banking
institutions.[25] There are five commercial banks,
whose branches are located throughout the country.

There are a number of special banks which have
been established in recent years. The Korean Reconstruction Bank lends to industry and handles long-
term foreign capital. The National Agricultural Co-
operative Federation lends to farmers, while the
Central Federation of Fisheries Cooperatives specialize in loans to the fishing industry. The Medium
Industry Bank lends to businesses of relatively small
scale. The Citizens National Bank maintains rotating
mujin accounts, which are very similar to open-end
mutual funds in the United States, and caters to consumer and small businesses.[26] The Korea Exchange
Bank finances mainly exports and imports, and the
Korea Housing Bank finances multifamily and commercial
building constructions. Other financial institutions,
which play a minor role, include postal savings, trust
funds, life insurance companies, and fire and casualty
insurance companies.

The relative importance of financial institutions
can be measured through a flow-of-funds analysis. The
flow-of-funds accounts are designed to provide a statistical framework appropriate to the analysis of
problems involving relationships among financial and
nonfinancial developments and to permit the tieing
together of sector- and financial-market analysis

into an integrated analysis for the economy as a
whole.[27]

Table 5.4 gives a summary statement of the flow-
of-funds matrix for 1964. Corporations are the only
deficit sector while all other sectors are surplus
sectors. Three important items in the financial account of the table are securities, foreign claims,
and loans. The total amount of securities issued
during 1964 was 6.8 billion won, mainly by corporations. Of this amount, 1.2 billion were purchased
by the financial sector and 3.5 billion by the government sector. The individual sector sold 0.8 billion. This means that the government owned a majority of securities issued during the year. The foreign
sector played an important role as a source of funds.
It provided 1.8 billion to the financial sector, 4.3
billion to the government sector, and 1.8 billion to
the private sector.

As mentioned before, a majority of loans went
to the public sector and publicly recommended businesses. In terms of the sources of funds for these
loans, borrowings from financial institutions and the
government played a greater role than time-and-savings
deposits. For instance, special and commercial loans,
the largest single item in the uses of funds by the
financial sector, amounted to 7.8 billion won. But
the financial sector borrowed 5 billion from financial
institutions themselves and the government sector and
only 3.3 billion from the private sector in the form
of time-and-savings deposits. The volume of time-and-
savings deposits increased sharply after the interest-
rate reform of 1965.

The relative role of financial intermediaries
can also be analyzed in terms of stock of financial
assets and liabilities as against the flow of funds.
The figures in Table 5.5 show that the nonfinancial
sectors had 606.7 billion won of primary securities
outstanding which were mainly issued by corporations.
Of this amount, the nonfinancial sectors, particularly the government and foreign sectors, owned a larger
part of primary securities, amounting to 375.7 billion. Financial institutions held the relatively small

TABLE 5.4

Summary Statement of Flow of Funds, 1964
(in billions of won)

	Financial Institutions Use	Source	Government Use	Source	Corporations Use	Source	Individuals Use	Source	Foreign Use	Source	Total[a] Use	Source
Nonfinancial Account												
Saving	-	1.9	-	34.9	-	20.1	-	30.7	-	5.2	-	92.7
Investment	1.0	-	21.2	-	43.0	-	25.0	-	-	-	92.7	-
Surplus or deficit	0.9	-	13.7	-	-22.9	-	5.7	-	5.2	-	-	-
Financial Account												
Surplus or deficit	-	0.9	-	13.7	-	-22.9	-	5.7	-	5.2	-	-
Money	-0.2	5.8	0.3	-0.4	-0.4	-	6.7	-	-	-	5.8	5.8
Deposit with BOK[b]	0.04	4.9	4.8	-	-	-	-	-	-	-	4.9	4.9
Time and saving deposits	-0.03	3.3	0.4	-	0.3	-	2.7	-	-	-	3.3	3.3
Insurance and trust	0.1	1.6	3.5	0.5	0.2	-	1.3	-	-	-	1.6	1.6
Securities	1.2	0.1	-	1.7	2.9	7.2	-0.8	-	-	-	6.8	6.8
BOK loans[b]	1.0	-	-	-	-	-0.7	-	-	-	-	1.0	1.0
Special and comm. loans	7.8	0.1	-	0.5	-	5.1	-	2.2	-	-	7.8	7.8
Ins. and trust loans	0.8	-	-	0.02	-	0.1	-	0.7	-	-	0.8	0.8
Other loans	0.2	-	-	-	-	3.2	3.2	0.2	-	-	3.4	3.4
Government loans	-	4.9	4.9	-	-	-	-	-	-	-	4.9	4.9
Subscriptions	-	0.3	1.3	-	0.2	1.2	-0.03	-	-	-	1.5	1.5
Trade credit	-	-	-1.5	0.8	8.6	4.3	-	2.0	-	-	7.1	7.1
Gold and foreign exchange	0.05	-	-	-	-	-	-	-	-	-	-	-
Foreign claims	-	1.8	0.2	4.3	-	1.8	-	-	7.9	0.2	8.1	8.1
Miscellaneous	8.4	1.7	-1.8	-2.4	4.1	14.0	2.7	-	-	-	13.3	13.3
Adjustment	-	-6.1	-	-6.6	-	2.7	-	4.9	-	2.5	-	-
Total	19.4	19.4	11.5	11.5	15.8	15.8	15.7	15.7	7.9	7.9	70.4	70.4

[a]Total figures include statistical discrepancy.

[b]Bank of Korea.

Source: Economic Statistics Yearbook (Bank of Korea, 1967).

TABLE 5.5

Financial Assets and Liabilities, 1966

(in billions of won)

Financial Claims	Financial Sector	Nonfinancial Sectors				
		Government	Corporations	Individuals	Foreign Sector	Totals
Assets						
Gold and foreign exchange	65.1	–	–	–	–	65.1
Primary securities[a]	231.0	114.8	51.5	89.5	119.9	606.7
Securities	19.8	31.7	12.3	69.6	–	–
Loans	211.2	83.1	39.2	19.9	–	–
Indirect securities[b]	2.6	29.8	20.9	110.6	–	163.8
Total	298.7	144.6	72.4	200.1	119.9	835.6
Liabilities						
Gold and foreign exchange	–	–	–	–	65.1	65.1
Primary securities	89.5	80.9	341.9	87.5	7.0	606.7
Securities	7.7	17.9	108.0	–	–	–
Loans	81.8	63.0	233.9	87.5	7.0	–
Indirect securities	163.8	–	–	–	–	163.8
Total	253.3	80.9	341.9	87.5	72.1	835.6

[a]Primary securities, in the language of John Gurley and his associates, include government bonds, corporate debentures, stocks, business loans, debts of consumers, and foreign claims. See John Gurley, et al., The Financial Structure of Korea (Bank of Korea, 1965), pp. 71–105.

[b]Indirect securities is a term covering demand deposits, time-and-savings deposits, and other short-term liquid claims.

Source: Economic Statistics Yearbook (Bank of Korea, 1968).

174

remainder of 231 billion.[28] The financial sector had
issued what is termed "indirect" securities of a little less than the amount of primary debt. The relative amount of indirect securities in relation to
primary debt in Korea is much smaller than that in
financially advanced countries. The indirect securities in Table 5.5 were held by the government and the
private sector, mostly by the latter. In order to
increase the participation of financial intermediaries
in the financing of the private sector, the share of
indirect securities held by the private sector should
be encouraged.

Interest Reform

One of the very important ways of diverting savings from the unofficial market (hoarding and even
perhaps consumption) is the establishment of attractive interest rates on indirect securities. Changes
in interest rates did not play a significant role in
attracting hidden savings until the interest reform
of October, 1965. In 1957, for instance, the average
interest rate on time-and-savings deposits was 12 percent, while the rates in the curb market ranged between 7 percent and 10 percent per month.[29] The gap
between the commercial-bank rates and the curb market
continued to exist until the interest reform, although
the spread between the rates changed from year to
year. Furthermore, as shown in Table 5.6, the official interest rates had not been attractive enough to
savers, because real interest rates adjusted for price
increases were either very low or negative until 1965.

Under the reform of that year, the ceilings on
both deposit and lending rates were raised substantially. Interest rates on time-and-savings deposits
were raised from 9 percent to 18 percent for 3-month
deposits and from 15 percent to 30 percent for 12-
month deposits. The Bank of Korea's rediscount rate
on commercial bills was raised from 11.5 percent to
21 percent and that on other securities from 16 percent to 23 percent. The commercial banks' maximum
discount rate on commercial bills was raised from 14
percent per annum to 24 percent and that secured by
other evidence of indebtedness from 16 percent to 26
percent.[30]

TABLE 5.6

Real Interest Rates, Financial Savings, and Gross National Product
(in billions of won)

Year	Time and Savings Deposits[a]	Official Interest Rate[b]	Wholesale Price Index[c]	Real Financial Savings[d]	Real Interest Rate[e]	Real GNP[f]
1957	1.5	12	94.1	1.6	–	522.7
1958	1.9	12	88.2	2.1	18.3	551.7
1959	5.5	10	90.3	6.1	7.6	575.8
1960	5.7	10	100.3	5.7	-0.7	589.1
1961	9.1	15	113.2	8.1	2.8	613.6
1962	16.8	15	123.8	13.5	5.6	634.9
1963	17.3	15	149.3	11.7	-5.6	693.0
1964	20.3	15	201.1	10.1	-19.7	750.3
1965	39.0	30[g]	221.2	17.6	20.0	805.9
1966	85.0	30	238.0	35.7	22.4	913.8
1967	128.9	30	252.2	51.1	23.6	990.9
1968	255.5	27	272.6	93.7	18.9	1,127.3

[a]The sum of savings deposits, notice deposits, time deposits, and installment savings deposits with all banking institutions at the end of the year indicated.
[b]Payable on deposit of twelve months and longer. Figures are given in percent.
[c]1960 = 100.
[d]In 1960 prices.
[e]official interest rate minus percentage change in wholesale price index.
[f]in 1965 prices.
[g]Effective October, 1965.
Source: Economic Statistics Yearbook (Bank of Korea, 1965, 1967, 1967, 1969).

The main purposes of the reform were, first, to
channel individual savings to financial intermediaries, and, second, to promote confidence in financial institutions. Although it is difficult to quan-
tify exactly the impact of the interest reform on
financial savings--owing to the use of a semicompul-
sory form of savings out of salaries and remittances
from abroad--time-and-savings deposits have increased
substantially since 1965. They doubled in 1966 and
continued to advance in 1967 and 1968 at a rate in
excess of the real GNP growth rate.

The interest reform was also intended to serve
as a clear-cut demonstration of the government's determination to curb inflation. The real interest
rate in fact averaged about 21 percent per annum in
1965-68. Slowly, savers began to feel some confidence
that savings at financial institutions would not be
taxed away by inflation.

In spite of its successes, the interest reform
contained some defects. Mainly, these concern interest charges on loans. First, rates on loans were set
lower than rates on deposits. Therefore, some corporations and individuals borrowed funds from banks and
deposited them in time-and-savings accounts at higher
rates, and many inefficient firms borrowed at the
relatively low rates. Consequently, the Monetary
Board set the rates on loans 1 percent higher in June,
1969. But the 1-percent differential is not still
wide enough.[31] Eligibility for preferential interest
rates on loans financing exports, agriculture, forestry, and fishery is somewhat vague, and the excessive
demand for loanable funds has contributed to continued
inflation. Because profit incentives are not at work
in banking under the present structure of interest
rates, efficiency at banks is not being encouraged.

Second, a disparity between interest rates on
domestic loans and foreign borrowing exists. The
average interest rate on foreign borrowing ranges between 6 percent and 10 percent.[32] Debt financing is
already advantageous to corporations because interest
paid on borrowed funds is deductible before arriving
at the taxable income which is subject to tax at a

corporate tax rate of around 40 percent.[33] On top of
this, foreign debt is much cheaper than domestic borrowing in financing corporate investment. The enormous increase in the demand for foreign loans has
added to domestic monetary expansion.[34] A normalization of the interest structure[35] may have to wait
until financial stability is firmly enough established
to permit a lowering of domestic rates and until loans
are curtailed to inefficient firms which speculate in
real estate with bank borrowings.

Other Financial Techniques

Besides the normalization of the interest structure, the following list of financial techniques exem-
plifies ways of increasing domestic savings. The list
contains major recommendations made by Gurley and his
associates and by the Korean Economist Association but
not yet implemented for action by the government.[36]

1. There should be an escalator clause,
   geared to the rate of inflation in
   demand deposits and in insurances and
   annuity contracts.

2. Certificates of time deposits (CD's)
   and short-term government bonds with
   various maturities and degrees of
   negotiability may be used.

3. Special financial institutions to attract hoardings in the agricultural
   sector may be established.

4. Government agencies such as the Korean
   Reconstruction Bank may issue their
   own debentures.

5. Government stockholdings in various
   financial institutions and industrial
   corporations should be sold to the
   private sector.

6. The stock market should be broadened
   by opening up family-controlled, closed
   corporations.

FISCAL TECHNIQUES

Firm tax policy is another method to mobilize
savings for investment. In fact, the IBRD Mission
to Korea suggested that fiscal policy should play a
major role in mobilizing domestic financial resources
because of uncertainties inherent in financial techniques to promote private savings. While taxes are
to some extent collected at the expense of private
investment and not only of consumption, there is a
net gain in investment if the revenues obtained are
devoted to capital formation rather than government-
consumption expenditures. Large public investments
in social-overhead capital are needed in Korea.

The scope of government-development activities
has in fact expanded greatly in recent years although
counterpart funds from foreign aid have declined.
Government revenues have been enlarged through increased taxes. As Table 5.7 shows, government revenues have increased substantially in absolute terms
since 1961 and also relative to GNP, although that
ratio has fluctuated somewhat.

It is interesting to note that the proportion
of revenues to GNP fell considerably during the high-
ly inflationary years 1963-64. The reasons for this
strong inverse relationship are not clear. It is
possible that the tax structure is regressive with
respect to inflation and that lags in tax payments
are especially damaging to government revenue in inflation.[37] Although the Korean tax system as a
whole is on a reasonably "current" basis, there still
is a lag between the time a tax liability is incurred
and the time of actual collection. Thus, in periods
of extremely rapid price increases such as in 1963-
64, revenues might have tended "to reflect tax liabilities based on somewhat lower prices."[38]

Furthermore, if the differential rates of sectoral growth during periods of rapid inflation have
the effect of increasing the relative importance of
those sectors subject to lower, effective tax rates,
public revenues may have increased less than would
have been the case under more stable conditions. An
unsophisticated tax system, which includes taxes on

volume rather than value of products (as in the case
of liquor) contributes to such a result.[39]

TABLE 5.7

Government Revenue, Gross National Product,
and Price Inflation
(in billions of won)

Year	Current Revenues[a]		Direct and Indirect Taxes		Percent of Change of Wholesale Price
	Amount	Percent of GNP	Amount	Percent of GNP	
1961	38.1	12.8	25.8	8.7	13.2
1962	48.5	13.9	33.5	9.6	9.4
1963	57.4	11.8	38.2	7.8	20.6
1964	68.2	9.8	46.0	6.6	34.7
1965	91.2	11.3	65.6	8.1	10.0
1966	137.6	13.3	102.8	10.0	7.6
1967	169.7	13.6	119.0	9.6	6.8
1968	248.1	15.7	183.8	11.7	8.1

[a]Current revenues include direct and indirect taxes
plus other revenues such as government monopoly
profits and tariff revenues.

Source: Economic Statistics Yearbook (Bank of Korea,
1965, 1967, 1969); International Bank for
Reconstruction and Development Mission to
Korea (January, 1968).

The ratio of taxes to GNP has increased since
1964, not only because price increases have been
relatively small but also because tax collection has
been improved. The Korean Government decided that a
major revenue increase could be achieved through full
enforcement of existing tax laws. It therefore concentrated its efforts on the reform of tax administration. A new administrative agency, the National

Taxation Office, was created in July, 1966, to cen-
tralize all tax-collection functions.[40] In order to
improve income reporting, tax-assessment criteria
based on sampling surveys of corporate and individual
earnings (differentiated according to size and loca-
tion of establishments) were used. Tax evaders were
charged with a criminal offense, and heavy penalties
were imposed.

Tax Policies for the Future

     In spite of this progress, there is still ample
room for further improvement. It may take a long
time, however, before tax practices in Korea will ap-
proximate U.S. standards. Meanwhile, tax revenues
may have to be increased by broadening the tax base
and by raising present tax rates. Some suggestions
follow:

1. Coordination of information on tax-
   payers' reports obtained from various
   sources.[41]

2. Eventual abolition of exemptions and
   deductions offered to export and other
   preferred industries.

3. Income taxes--at present, maximum personal tax rate is 50 percent on annual
   incomes of 80,000 won or more; maximum
   corporate tax rate is 35 percent on
   public corporations and 45 percent on
   closed corporations with annual incomes
   of 5 million won or more.[42] Income
   bracket schedules and tax rates could
   both be raised to reach more of the
   upper-income classes. As a result of
   rapid economic growth and of inflation,
   top brackets of personal and corporate
   incomes no longer imply the same degree
   of progressivity as before.

4. Heavier taxation of urban lands and
   buildings to discourage speculation in
   real estate.

5. Heavier taxation of individual consumption of petroleum, alcohol, ciga-
rettes, and other nonessentials.

6. Increase of revenues from tariffs.

In conclusion, government policies have correctly arrived at increased investments and savings.
Investment strategy in export and manufacturing industries and in social-overhead capital has been appropriate. Financial and fiscal policies have been
relatively successful. But more difficult tasks remain for the future, particularly in achieving sustained financial stability and in effective tax collections. The exposure of Korean Government officials
to the tax administration of advanced countries, such
as the United States, has been of great aid, as has
been the program to educate the Korean people on the
importance of paying taxes to finance development.

In summary, achieving the high marginal-savings
rate set out in our projection is a difficult task,
although the savings rate has shown a rising trend
in recent years. The ultimate achievement will depend on successful anti-inflationary policies, progress in the financial intermediation process, and
fiscal-policy rationalization as outlined in this
chapter.

In addition, maintaining a relatively stable
capital-output ratio will also depend on the successful implementation of investment plans discussed
early in this chapter. The investment plans should
be consistently carried out, even though the political party changes in different regimes.

NOTES

1. Robert Nathan Associates, An Economic Program for Korean Reconstruction (United Nations Korean
Reconstruction Agency, 1954), pp. 1-5.

2. Ibid., p. 389.

3. Joe Won Lee, "Planning Efforts for Economic
Development," in J. S. Chung, ed., Patterns of Economic Development: Korea (Detroit: Cellar Book Shop,
1966), pp. 1-5.

4. Ibid., pp. 1-9.

5. Charles Wolf, "Economic Planning in Korea,"
Asian Survey (December, 1962), pp. 22-27.

6. Ibid., p. 23; David Cole and Y. W. Nam,
"The Pattern and Significance of Economic Planning
in Korea" (Mimeographed); paper presented at the
Conference on Korean Planning, Northwestern University, June, 1968), p. 14.

7. Summary of the First Five-Year Economic
Plan (1962-66) (Seoul: Republic of Korea, 1962), p.
25.

8. Ibid., p. 33.

9. See Holger Engberg, "Frency Money and Capital Markets and Monetary Management," The Bulletin
(New York University Graduate School of Business Administration, January-March, 1965), pp. 4-5.

10. Summary of the First Five-Year Plan, op.
cit., pp. 177-79.

11. Ibid., pp. 79-89.

12. Irma Adelman, et al., "The Korean Sectoral
Model" (Mimeographed); paper presented at the Confer-
ence on Korean Planning, Northwestern University,
June, 1968, pp. 3-9.

13. The Second Five-Year Economic Development
Plan (1967-71) (Seoul: Government of the Republic of
Korea, 1966), p. 84.

14. Ibid.

15. Lee, op. cit., pp. 1.5-1.6.

16. For the relevant arguments see Ragner Nurske, _Equilibrium and Growth in the World Economy_ (Cambridge: Harvard University Press, 1961), pp. 51-55; and Robert B. Sutcliffe, "Balanced and Unbalanced Growth," _Quarterly Journal of Economics_ (November, 1964), pp. 621-40.

17. John Gurley and E. S. Shaw, "Financial Intermediaries and Savings-Investment Process," _Journal of Finance_ (May, 1956), pp. 257-76; John Gurley and E. S. Shaw, "Financial Structure and Economic Development," _Economic Development and Social Change_ (April, 1967), pp. 257-68; and Hugh T. Patrick, "Financial Development and Economic Growth in Under-developed Countries," _Economic Development and Cultural Change_ (January, 1966), pp. 174-89.

18. John Gurley, _The Financial Structure of Korea_ (Seoul: Bank of Korea, 1965), p. 1.

19. _A Program to Mobilize Domestic Capital_ (Seoul: Korean Economists Association, 1965), pp. 14-17.

20. Gurley, _The Financial Structure of Korea_, op. cit., p. 5.

21. _Stabilization and Program Progress_ (United Nations Command, Office of Economic Coordination for Korea, 1958), p. 29.

22. Arthur I. Bloomfield, _A Report and Recommendations on Monetary Policy and Banking in Korea_ (Seoul: Bank of Korea, 1965), pp. 105-6.

23. _Economic Survey: 1967_ (Seoul: Economic Planning Board, 1968), pp. 9-10.

24. Gurley, _The Financial Structure of Korea_, op. cit., p. 81.

25. _Ibid._, p. 8.

26. _Ibid._

27. Lawrence Ritter, "The Flow-of-Funds Account: A New Approach to Financial Market Analysis," Journal of Finance (May, 1963), pp. 219-28.

28. Gurley, The Financial Structure of Korea, op. cit., pp. 44-46.

29. Charles Wolf, On Aspects of Korea's Five-Year Development Plan (Seoul: Ministry of Reconstruction, 1961), pp. 25-27.

30. International Financial News Survey (Washington, D.C.: International Monetary Fund, October 22, 1965).

31. Hankook Ilbo (Korean daily newspaper, Seoul, June 1, 1969).

32. Economic Survey: 1967, op. cit., p. 8.

33. A Study on Legal Entity Tax in Korea (Seoul: Korean Economic Development Institute, 1966), pp. 48-54.

34. S. Kanesa-Thasan, "Stabilizing An Economy --The Korean Experience," a paper presented at the Conference on Korean Planning, Northwestern University, June 19-21, 1968, p. 15.

35. The IBRD mission to Korea in January, 1968.

36. See Gurley, The Financial Structure of Korea, op. cit., pp. 105-6; and A Program to Mobilize Domestic Capital, op. cit., pp. 65-66.

37. Robert H. Johnson, "Tax Policies for the Second Five-Year Economic Development Plan," in Nathan Product Series (Seoul: Economic Planning Board, 1965), pp. 178-79.

38. Ibid.

39. Ibid.

40. Economic Survey: 1967, op. cit., pp. 36-37.

41. Johnson, op. cit., pp. 180-81.

42. Hankook Ilbo, op. cit., August 1, 1968;
and the IBRD mission to Korea in January, 1968.

CHAPTER **6** SUMMARY AND
CONCLUSIONS

THE IMPORTANCE OF EXTERNAL CAPITAL

Korea has experienced consistent economic growth
since 1953 and rapid economic development since 1962.
Foreign capital has been the main source of such
growth, and the internal and external gaps have tended to narrow in recent years, as exports and domestic
savings have increased sharply in order to finance
not only import as well as investment requirements
but also external-debt services.

In evaluating the effects of foreign capital on
economic growth, the incremental capital-output ratio
(ICOR) is again used to estimate the contribution of
foreign capital. Actual growth rate with the help of
foreign capital can be compared with the likely ex
ante growth rate without the inflow of foreign capital. In other words, total investment requirements
are financed by domestic savings alone. The actual
growth rate of GNP averaged 7.4 percent in 1957-68.
The average ICOR (k) is 2.4 as indicated in Table
2.8, while the average savings rate (s) is 6.8 percent as shown in Table 2.9. If total investment were
financed solely by domestic savings, the average
growth rate (r) would have been only 2.9 percent without the help of foreign capital.* The difference between the actual growth rate of 7.4 percent and the
possible ex ante growth rate of 2.9 percent may well
be considered as the net contribution made by foreign
capital.

---

*It is derived from the formula, $r = s/k =
6.8/2.4 = 2.9$.

It is true that foreign capital has played an
important role in Korea's economic development. But
foreign aid in the form of grants before 1962 had
been used mainly for military defense and consumer
goods, particularly food, during the Korean War and
reconstruction periods.[1] Foreign loans and direct
investment since 1962, on the other hand, have been
used mainly for investment projects. Private loans
were concentrated mainly in such fields as chemicals,
cement, and textile manufacturing, while public loans
were mainly for social-overhead capital such as electricity, railways, waterworks, and drainage systems.
Direct investments were concentrated mainly in the
electronics, food processing, and fertilizer industries.[2] Consequently, foreign loans and direct investment have contributed greatly to the capital formation.

Not only the introduction of foreign loans but
also the construction of various investment projects
have made great strides, with remarkable effects on
exports and import substitution. An accelerated and
dramatic increase in exports has taken place since
1964. There are many reasons to believe that the
investments in import-substitute industries have just
begun to yield their fruits.

KOREA'S ABILITY TO PAY BACK ITS EXTERNAL DEBT

The total amount of external-capital needs in
Korea is estimated to be $3.9 billion during the pro-
jection period (1967-76). Although the bulk of foreign capital consists of foreign loans, our projection concludes that the burden of debt service will
not reach a danger point and that Korea will be able
to pay back external debts in the long run if the
assumptions underlying the parameter estimates are
reasonable. Annual gross borrowings reach a peak of
$290 million in 1970 and then decline each year, but
cumulative outstanding debt continues to increase at
a decreasing rate. Both the internal and external
gaps decline after 1967. This means that domestic
savings will finance an increasing part of investment requirements and that the increase in exports

will not only finance an increasing part of import
requirements but will assume the repayment of external debt.

Although this study makes a favorable conclusion
on Korea's ability to pay back its external debts, it
does not mean that Korea will be free of debt-service
problems. As stated in the sensitivity analysis in
Chapter 2, the amount of external-capital needs will
increase if some relevant parameters such as the export growth rate, savings rate, and amortization
period decrease, or if the incremental capital-output
ratio, the import coefficient and the interest rate
on external debt increases in the future. To put the
argument differently, the burden of external debt will
increase if foreign capital is not efficiently managed but is used for unproductive projects, such as
for political and shortsighted speculative purposes,
and thereby some of the assumed parameter values are
not realized in the future.

The assumptions on the future parameters are
based on the notion that the Korean Government, which
plays a significant role in all phases of economic
activities, will continue to reform the ineffective
system and introduce economically sound policies. The
Foreign Capital Inducement Law must be continued, and
more lenient treatment can be given to foreign firms
in their business tax and tariff payments.

Tax exemptions and interest subsidies should be
raised for the export industry of labor-intensive
manufactured goods, particularly for the industry
with a high exchange-earnings rate. High protective
tariffs are justified for the import-substitute industry. This does not mean that export subsidies and
protective tariffs should be permanent. For the promotion of an economic system based on incentives,
they should be gradually abolished as the export- and
import-substitute industries become competitive in
the long run. Furthermore, the establishment of a
more realistic exchange rate is suggested in this
study, in order to encourage exports and to eliminate
windfall profits from imports under the overvalued
exchange rate.

Finally, achieving the high marginal-savings rate set out in our projection will ultimately depend on successful anti-inflationary policies, progress in the financial intermediation process, and fiscal-policy rationalization. Maintaining a relatively stable capital-output ratio will _also_ depend on the successful implementation of investment plans.

FOR FURTHER RESEARCH

The author's suggestions for further research concerning foreign-capital needs in Korea are: first, a sectoral study for estimating external-capital needs and, second, an evaluation of investment projects financed by foreign capital.

Sectoral models may give a better picture of foreign-capital needs in a number of sectors of the economy if a functional relationship of a sector can be specified by nonlinear forms with multiple-sectoral variables. A sectoral study will, therefore, require computer facilities and time. The projection of foreign-capital needs can be improved if the result of an aggregate model is compared with that of a sectoral model. Owing to limited time and financial resources, an aggregate model has been employed in this study. The aggregate model is rather crude and uses simple linear functions.

The current headlines of Korean newspapers are frequently concerned with government investigations of companies financed by foreign capital. Recently, a number of companies which had borrowed heavily from abroad failed because of financial difficulties. An analysis of investment projects is needed according to the capital-budgeting method based on cost-benefit criteria. To be more explicit, an investment project should be evaluated as to whether the rate of return on investment is greater than the cost of foreign capital, or the value of the investment discounted to the present is greater than the total cost of investment. In the case of Korea, neither the internal rate-of-return method nor the discounted cash-flow method is used as an investment criterion.

NOTES

1.   See <u>Monthly Statistical Review</u> (Seoul: Bank of Korea, December, 1962), p. 5.

2.   <u>Economic Survey, 1967</u> (Seoul: Economic Planning Board, 1968), pp. 58-59.

BIBLIOGRAPHY

BIBLIOGRAPHY

Books

Avramovic, D. Debt Servicing Capacity and Postwar
    Growth in International Indebtedness. Baltimore:
    Johns Hopkins Press, 1958.

_____. Economic Growth and External Debt.
    Baltimore: Johns Hopkins Press, 1964.

_____, and R. Gulhati. Debt Servicing Problems
    of Low-Income Countries. Baltimore: Johns
    Hopkins Press, 1960.

Buchanan, Norman S., and Howard S. Ellis. Approaches
    to Economic Development. New York: The
    Twentieth Century Fund, 1955.

Cho, Ki Jun. History of Korean Economy. Seoul:
    Pommunsa, 1962.

Choi, Ho Jin. An Outline of Korean Economic History.
    Seoul: Pommungok, 1962.

Clark, Colin. Conditions of Economic Growth. Third
    edition. London: Macmillan, 1951.

Domar, Evsey D. Essays in the Theory of Economic
    Growth. New York: Oxford University Press,
    1957.

Haberler, G. The Theory of International Trade.
    New York: The Macmillan Co., 1936.

Harrod, R. F. Towards a Dynamic Economics. London:
    Macmillan & Co., 1963.

195

Hirschman, Albert D. The Strategy of Economic De-
    velopment. New Haven: Yale University Press,
    1958.

Johnson, Harry. Economic Policies Toward Less De-
    veloped Countries. Washington, D.C.: The
    Brookings Institution, 1967.

Kindleberger, Charles P. Foreign Trade and the
    National Economy. New Haven: Yale University
    Press, 1962.

_____. International Economics. Homewood,
    Ill.: Richard D. Irwin, Inc., 1963.

Krooss, Herman E. American Economic Development.
    Englewood, N.J.: Prentice-Hall, Inc., 1966.

Kuznets, Simon. Modern Economic Growth. New Haven:
    Yale University Press, 1966.

Lary, Hal. Imports of Manufactures from Less De-
    veloped Countries. New York: National Bureau
    of Economic Research, 1968.

League of Nations. Industrialization and Foreign
    Trade. Geneva: 1945.

Leibenstein, Harvey. Economic Backwardness and
    Economic Growth. New York: John Wiley & Sons,
    Inc., 1963.

Lewis, W. Arthur. Development Planning. New York:
    Harper & Row, 1966.

_____. The Theory of Economic Growth. London:
    George Allen & Unwin, 1955.

Linder, Staffan Burenstam. An Essay on Trade and
    Transformation. New York: John Wiley, 1961.

_____. Trade and Trade Policy for Development.
    New York: Frederick A. Praeger, 1967.

Mikesell, F. Foreign Exchange in the Postwar World.
    New York: The Twentieth Century Fund, 1954.

Nurske, Ragner. Equilibrium and Growth in the World
    Economy. Cambridge: Harvard University Press,
    1961.

_____ . Patterns of Trade and Development.
    Oxford: Basil Blackwell, 1961.

_____ . Problems of Capital Formation in
    Underdeveloped Countries. New York: Oxford
    University Press, 1961.

Pincus, John. Trade, Aid, and Development. New York:
    McGraw-Hill, 1967.

Schlesinger, E. Multiple Exchange Rates and Economic
    Development. Princeton, N.J.: Department of
    Economics, Princeton University, 1954.

Schott, Francis. The Evolution of Latin American
    Exchange Rate Policies Since World War II.
    Princeton, N.J.: Department of Economics,
    Princeton University, 1959.

Singer, H. W. International Development. New York:
    McGraw-Hill, 1964.

Sohmen, E. Flexible Exchange Rates. Chicago:
    University of Chicago Press, 1961.

Triffin, Robert. Gold and the Dollar Crisis. New
    Haven: Yale University Press, 1961.

Vanek, Jaroslav. Estimating Foreign Resource Needs
    for Economic Development. New York: McGraw-
    Hill, 1967.

Viner, Jacob. Studies in the Theory of International
    Trade. New York: Reprinted by Augustus M.
    Kelley, Publisher, 1965.

Articles

Alter, G. M. "The Servicing of Foreign Capital
   Inflows by Underdeveloped Countries." In
   Economic Development for Latin America, edited
   by H. S. Ellis and H. C. Wallich. New York:
   Macmillan & Co., 1963.

Balassa, Bela. "An Empirical Demonstration of the
   Classical Comparative Cost Theory," Review of
   Economics and Statistics (August, 1963).

_____. "Tariff Protection in Industrial
   Countries: An Evaluation," Journal of Political
   Economy (December, 1965).

Burgard, H. "External Impact on Economic Development,"
   Kyklos, XX (1967).

Cairncross, A. K. "Capital Formation in Take-off."
   In Economics of Take-off into Sustained Growth,
   edited by W. W. Rostow. New York: St. Martin's
   Press, 1963.

Chenery, Hollis B. "Patterns of Industrial Growth,"
   The American Economic Review (September, 1960).

_____, and A. M. Strout. "Foreign Assistance
   and Economic Development," The American Economic
   Review (September, 1966).

Corden, W. H. "The Structure of a Tariff System and
   the Effective Protective Rate," Journal of
   Political Economy (June, 1966).

Davis, Tom E. "Inflation and Growth in Latin
   America," Economic Development and Cultural
   Change (July, 1966).

Diaz-Alexandro, C. F. "On the Import Intensity of
   Import Substitution," Kyklos, XVIII (1965).

Dorrance, Graeme S. "The Effect of Inflation on
   Economic Development," IMF Staff Papers
   (March, 1963).

Engberg, Holger. "French Money and Capital Markets
    and Monetary Management," The Bulletin, New York
    University Graduate School of Business Adminis-
    tration (January-March 1965).

Fabricant, Solomon. "Basic Facts on Productivity
    Change." Occasional Paper 63. New York:
    National Bureau of Economic Research, Inc.

Fei, John C. H., and Douglas S. Paauw. "Foreign
    Assistance and Self-Help: A Reappraisal of
    Development Finance," The Review of Economics
    and Statistics (August, 1965).

Finch, David. "Investment Service of Underdeveloped
    Countries," IMF Staff Papers, 1951.

Grubel, H. G., and H. G. Johnson. "Nominal Tariffs,
    Indirect Taxes and Effective Rates of Protection,
    the Common Market Countries 1959," Economic
    Journal (December, 1967).

Gurley, John, and E. S. Shaw. "Financial Intermedi-
    aries and Savings-Investment Process," Journal
    of Finance (May, 1956).

_____. "Financial Structure and Economic
    Development," Economic Development and Social
    Change (April, 1967).

Hagen, E. E. "An Economic Justification of Protec-
    tionism," Quarterly Journal of Economics
    (November, 1958).

Humphrey, David B. "Note on Import Substitution:
    The Case of Brazil," The Journal of Development
    Studies (October, 1966).

Kenen, P. B., and E. B. Yudin. "The Demand for
    International Reserves," The Review of Economics
    and Statistics (August, 1965).

Krueger, A. D. "Balance of Payments Theory," Journal
    of Economic Literature (March, 1969).

Lee, Joe Won. "Planning Efforts for Economic Development." In Patterns of Economic Development: Korea, edited by J. S. Chung. Detroit: Cellar Book Shop, 1966.

Leff, N. H., and D. Netto. "Import Substitution, Foreign Investment, and International Disequilibrium," The Journal of Development Studies (April, 1966).

Leibenstein, Harvey. "The Incremental Capital-Output Ratio," Review of Economics and Statistics (February, 1966).

MacDougal, Donald. "British and American Exports: A Study Suggested by the Theory of Comparative Costs," Economic Journal (December, 1951).

McKinnon, R. I. "Foreign Exchange Constraints in Economic Development and Efficient Aid Allocation," The Economic Journal (June, 1964).

Merret, S. R., and J. S. Wabe. "A Modification of the Savings-Investment Approach to Devaluation," Oxford Economic Papers (November, 1964).

Myint, H. "The Classical Theory of International Trade and Underdeveloped Countries," Economic Journal (June, 1958).

Nurske, Ragner. "Conditions of International Equilibrium." In Readings in the Theory of International Trade, edited by H. S. Ellis and L. A. Metzler. Philadelphia: The Blakiston Co., 1949.

Patel, Surendra J., "A Note on the Incremental Capital-Output Ratio and Economic Growth in Developing Countries," Kyklos, XXI (1968).

Patrick, Hugh T. "Financial Development and Economic Growth in Underdeveloped Countries," Economic Development and Social Change (January, 1966).

Prebisch, R. "Commercial Policy in the Underdeveloped Countries," The American Economic Review (May, 1959).

_____. "Towards a New Trade Policy for Development," Proceedings of UNCTAD. Vol. II. New York: United Nations, 1964.

Ritter, Lawrence. "The Flow-of-Funds Account: A New Approach to Financial Market Analysis," Journal of Finance (May, 1963).

Rosenstein-Rodan, P. N. "International Aid for Underdeveloped Countries," The Review of Economics and Statistics (May, 1961).

Rostow, W. "The Take Off into Self-Sustaining Growth," Economic Journal (March, 1965).

Soligo, R., and J. Stern. "Tariff Protection, Import Substitution and Industrial Efficiency," Pakistan Development Review (Summer, 1965).

Stamp, Maxwell. "The Stamp Plan." In Compendium of Plans for International Monetary Reform, edited by Robert G. Hawkins. The Bulletin, No. 37-38. New York University Graduate School of Business Administration (December, 1965).

Sutcliffe, Robert B. "Balanced and Unbalanced Growth," Quarterly Journal of Economics (November, 1964).

Wolf, Charles. "Economic Planning in Korea," Asian Survey (December, 1962).

Korean Government Publications

Allocation of Foreign Exchanges for Imports. Seoul: Ministry of Commerce and Industry, 1968.

Economic Survey. Seoul: Economic Planning Board, 1967.

Economic White Paper. Seoul: Economic Planning Board, 1967.

Estimation of Import Substitutes. Seoul: Ministry of Commerce and Industry, 1967.

Foreign Capital Inducement Law. Seoul: Economic
    Planning Board, 1966.

Johnson, Robert H. "Tax Policies for the Second
    Five-Year Economic Development Plan." Nathan
    Product Series. Seoul: Economic Planning
    Board, 1965.

The Korean Trade Structure and Policies. Seoul:
    Ministry of Finance, 1967.

Musgrave, Peggy. Trade Targets and Policies in
    Korea's Economic Development. Seoul: Economic
    Planning Board, 1965.

Overall Resources Budget: 1968. Seoul: Economic
    Planning Board, 1968.

The Second Five-Year Economic Development Plan
    (1967-71). Seoul: Government of the Republic
    of Korea, 1966.

Significant Economic Indicators. Seoul: Economic
    Planning Board, 1967.

Summary of the First Five-Year Economic Plan (1962-
    66. Seoul: Republic of Korea, 1962.

The Status Report of Foreign Capital Inflow by
    Projects. Seoul: Economic Planning Board, 1967.

Tudor, Thomas H. "Export Promotion Measures."
    Nathan Product Series. Seoul: Economic Plan-
    ning Board, 1965.

Wolf, Charles. On Aspects of Korea's Five-Year
    Development Plan. Seoul: Ministry of Recon-
    struction, 1961.

Reports, Statistics, and Miscellaneous
Publications

Adelman, Irma, et al. "The Korean Sectoral Model."
    Paper presented at the Conference on Korean
    Planning, Northwestern University, June 19-21,
    1968. Mimeographed.

Bank of Korea Publications

    Annual Economic Review. Seoul, 1948.

    Balance of Payments of Korea. Seoul, 1967.

    Economic Statistics Yearbook. Seoul, 1959,
       1961, 1964, 1965, 1966, 1967, 1968, and 1969.

    IMF Consultation Mission. Seoul, 1962.

    Monthly Economic Statistics. November, 1969.

    Monthly Statistical Review. Seoul, February,
       1965; October, 1965; July, 1967; March, 1968.

    Price Statistics Summary. Seoul, 1966.

    A Report and Recommendations on Monetary Policy
       and Banking in Korea. (By Arthur I.
       Bloomfield.) Seoul, 1965.

    Review of Korean Economy, 1967. Seoul, 1968.

    Review of Korean Economy, 1968. Seoul, 1969.

Chao, Joseph T. C. "Taiwan's Economic Growth: A
    Case Study of Trade Expansion Policy." Un-
    published dissertation, New York University
    Graduate School of Business Administration, 1967.

Cole, David, and Y. W. Nam. "The Pattern and Sig-
    nificance of Economic Planning in Korea."
    Paper presented at the Conference on Korean
    Planning, Northwestern University, June, 1968.
    Mimeographed.

Economic Report of the President. Washington, D.C.:
    U.S. Government Printing Office, 1968.

Economist. (London), December 31, 1966.

Gurley, John, et al. The Financial Structure of
    Korea. Seoul: Bank of Korea, 1965.

Hankook Ilbo. Korean daily newspaper. Seoul, March
      15, 1968; March 27, 1968; April 16, 1968; May
      29, 1968; June 23, 1968; August 1, 1968; June
      1, 1969.

International Monetary Fund (IMF). International
      Financial News Survey. Washington, D.C.:
      October 22, 1965.

_____, and International Bank for Reconstruc-
      tion and Development (IBRD). Articles of
      Agreement. Washington, D.C.: 1944.

_____, Direction of Trade: Annals 1961-65.
      Washington, D.C., n.d.

Kanesa-Thasan, S. "Stabilizing an Economy--The
      Korean Experience." Paper presented at the
      Conference on Korean Planning, Northwestern
      University, June 19-21, 1968. Mimeographed.

Korean Economic Development Institute. Analyses of
      Capital Cost: Selected Industrial Establishments.
      Seoul, 1967.

_____. A Study on Legal Entity Tax in Korea.
      Seoul, 1966.

Korean Economists Association. A Program to Mobilize
      Domestic Capital. Seoul, 1965.

Korean Productivity Center. The Analysis on Substi-
      tute Effect of Import Substitute Industry.
      Seoul, 1965.

_____. Estimate of Labor Productivity in
      Korean Manufacturing. Seoul, 1967.

Korean Reconstruction Bank. Industrial Report.
      Seoul, 1966.

Korean Trade Association. Korean Export Industry.
      Seoul, 1968.

BIBLIOGRAPHY

Kuznets, P. W. "Korea's Five-Year Plans." Paper pre-
    sented at the Conference on Korean Planning,
    Northwestern University, June 19-21, 1968.
    Mimeographed.

New York Times, February 10, 1967.

Seoul Kyungje Shinmoon. Seoul daily economic news-
    paper, January 29, 1967.

Seoul National University. A Report on Import Sub-
    stitute Industry in Korea. Seoul, 1967.

Statistical Abstract of the United States. Washing-
    ton, D.C.: U.S. Government Printing Office,
    1967.

United Nations Publications

    Demographic Yearbook. New York, 1966.

    External Financing of Economic Development.
        New York, 1968.

    Final Act of GATT. Lake Success, N.Y.: 1947.

    Monthly Bulletin of Statistics. New York:
        December, 1967, June, 1968.

    Proceedings of the U.N. Conference on Trade and
        Development (UNCTAD). New York: IV, 1964;
        V, 1964.

    U.N. Statistical Yearbook. New York, 1966.

    Yearbook of National Accounts Statistics.
        New York, 1966.

United Nations Command, Office of Economic Coordina-
    tion for Korea. Stabilization and Program
    Progress. Seoul, 1958.

United Nations Economic Commission for Asia and the
    Far East (ECAFE). Review of Long-Term Economic
    Projections for Selected Countries in the ECAFE
    Region. Bangkok, 1964.

_____. "Import Substitution and Export
    Diversification." Economic Survey of Asia and
    the Far East. 1963.

United Nations Korean Reconstruction Agency (UNKRA).
    An Economic Program for Korean Reconstruction.
    Robert Nathan Associates, 1954.

Wu, H. C. Prewar and Postwar Trade Pattern of Korea.
    Washington, D.C.: International Monetary Fund
    (IMF), 1949.

ABOUT THE AUTHOR

Seung Hee Kim is Assistant Professor of Finance at the School of Commerce and Finance, Saint Louis University. Previously, he taught Money and Banking at the School of Commerce, New York University and International Economics at Canisius College. He has also worked in the International Banking Department, Manufacturers Hanover Trust Company in New York and was a Junior Fellow at the Center for International Studies, New York University.

Professor Kim was born in Korea and came to the United States in 1956. He received his B.S. degree from Juniata College in Pennsylvania and his M.B.A. and Ph.D. from the Graduate School of Business Administration, New York University.